GARDENERS'
QUESTIONS
ANSWERED

GARDENERS'
QUESTIONS
ANSWERED

RICHARD BIRD

a Salamander book

Published by Salamander Books Limited
LONDON

A SALAMANDER BOOK

Published by Salamander Books Ltd
129-137 York Way
London N7 9LG
United Kingdom

1 3 5 7 9 8 6 4 2

ISBN 0 86101 809 5

Managing Editor: Joanna Smith
Editorial and design: Ian Penberthy
Artwork: Julian Baker
Original design concept: Aardvark Design Studio Ltd
Colour separation: Classic Scan, Singapore
Printed in Spain

The publishers are grateful to both individuals and companies who have supplied the
photographs on the following pages:

Richard Bird: 1, 7, 8, 10, 12 left, 15, 16/17 bottom, 18, 22, 23, 27, 28, 56, 57, 58, 62 top, 65,
70/71 top left, 78
The Garden Picture Library: 3, 16 top, 20, 21, 25 top, 31, 32, 34, 35, 36, 38 left, 38/39, 42,
43, 44, 46, 49, 51, 59 left, 60 top, 61, 62 bottom, 63, 64, 67, 68, 71 top right and bottom, 72,
73 top, 75, 77
Giles Stokoe: 12/13 top, 55, 59 right, 60 bottom, 66
Clive Nichols: 19, 25 bottom, 30 (photograph taken at The Old School House, Essex), 45
Harry Smith Collection: 69, 73 bottom, 74

CONTENTS

INTRODUCTION

One aspect of being a gardening writer is that you are never off duty. Whenever anyone discovers what you do, they immediately ask a barrage of questions. This occurs as I travel around the country looking at gardens, when giving lectures, and when people visit my own garden. Even the supper table is not sacrosanct.

Many of the questions crop up time and time again, and it is these that I have presented in this book, in the hope that they will help solve the common problems that confront many gardeners. However, there is rarely only one answer to any question. Each garden is different in terms of soil and climate, and in what the gardener is trying to do. What works well in one garden may not in another. If you have found an effective way of doing something that is against current wisdom, carry on doing it your way.

Having said that, I hope that what follows will help to add to your knowledge, but do remember that real experience can only be obtained by getting your hands dirty. The more gardening you do, the more you will learn. Don't become too despondent at the loss of plants, the ravages of insects, or crippling drought. The advantage of an annual cycle in gardening means you can always start again the following year, learning from the mistakes of the previous one.

Richard Bird

Kilndown, Kent.

THE FLOWER GARDEN

I have heard that one way of attracting butterflies to the garden is to plant a Butterfly Bush (*Buddleja*), but are there any other flowers that have the same effect?

Various forms of wildlife will add an extra dimension to any garden, and none is more welcome than butterflies. As a general rule, many of the species and older plants are richer in nectar than the modern hybrids and cultivars, so they are more attractive to butterflies. An old-fashioned, cottage-garden style of planting is likely to produce the best results.

Among the plants that are worth using are the Stonecrops (*Sedum*) and members of the Daisy family. The latters' flower heads comprise many individual flowers, or florets, which usually are rich in nectar, so they make good butterfly plants. Michaelmas Daisies (*Aster*), Purple Cone Flower (*Echinacea*), *Erigeron*, the Sea Hollies (*Eryngium*), Tickseed (*Coreopsis*) and Golden Rod (*Solidago*) are all good examples. Mints (*Mentha*) are very good, as are the Catmints (*Nepeta*).

As well as garden plants, using native flora from the region is also a good way of attracting butterflies. These may be planted in the ordinary borders or in a part of the garden dedicated to wild flowers.

▼ A Comma butterfly enjoying the nectar provided by *Aster* 'King George'.

Left and right: Careful combination of colours makes a more satisfying picture than when they are arranged in a 'hit-or-miss' fashion.

Understanding the arrangement of the basic colour wheel will help when planning the colours of a border.

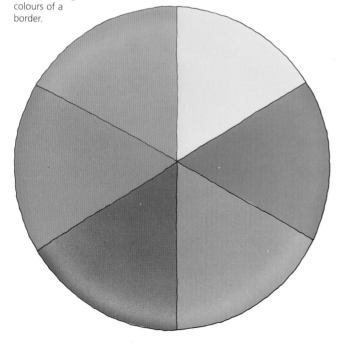

▲ **I am planning a new border, but I can't decide on a colour scheme. Which colours go well together?**

It is always more satisfying to arrange the colours of your flowers and foliage, than simply to dot them about at random. A spotty border creates a restless picture, while a border that contains drifts or groups of related colours is much more pleasing.

Bright colours are exciting, but can become tiring after a while, so use them sparingly. Soft colours, however, create a restful scene and can be used more extensively. Cool colours, such as the blues, form one of the most peaceful pictures, especially when combined with greens or purples, which are adjacent to blue on the colour wheel. A fresher, more lively effect can be created by moving further round the wheel and mixing blues with yellows or reds. If you choose the opposite colour - orange - you will create a very lively scene indeed.

These principles hold true for all starting points on the wheel: adjacent colours blend harmoniously, while opposites create a vivid contrast. Thus red and purple blend, while red and green stand out against each other. The most pleasing effects are created by using sympathetic colours with the occasional splash of a contrasting colour to catch the eye and add excitement.

I have tried growing Snowdrop bulbs that I have bought, but have never succeeded in getting them established, although they grow in other gardens near here. Can you suggest a reason for this?

It seems likely that you are buying dried bulbs that have been sold in a packet. These rarely succeed. You must plant Snowdrop bulbs while they are still fresh and their roots still alive. This can be at any time of year, although most gardeners do this 'in the green', that is after the bulbs have finished flowering, but still have their leaves. Although this is not the best time, it is convenient, as the leaves remind you to do the job and show you where the bulbs are to be found.

The optimum time to plant the bulbs is when they are dormant, but they should not be allowed to dry out; lift and replant them immediately. When purchasing Snowdrop bulbs, buy them in pots so that you can see that they are flourishing. Alternatively, some nurseries offer them 'in the green', the bulbs having been freshly dug up. Plant these out in the garden as soon as you get them home.

▲ Snowdrops are best transplanted at the time the flowers die down.

I am thinking of creating a rock garden. Can you tell me what type of rock would be best?

There is no hard-and-fast rule as to what constitutes the best rock for a rock garden, but most gardeners agree that for the best effect it should be stone that is native to the area. For example in a region where sandstone is the predominant rock, limestone will look out of place. Local rock is also cheaper, as it reduces transport costs.

Harder rocks, such as granite, should be avoided, as their texture and general appearance is not sympathetic. Don't use soft stone that crumbles in the frosts; remember, however, that some sandstones are soft when they are first quarried, but they harden after exposure to the air.

Plastic imitation rock has very little to recommend it, as it rarely looks realistic, while pieces of old concrete will never appear anything other than what they are.

This shady corner is given a luxuriant feeling by the careful use of cool greens and creams. ▶

My garden faces north and is rather shady. Which flowers can I grow in it?

A surprising number of plants can be grown in shade, although unfortunately, they are generally not as brightly coloured as those that prefer full sun. Many are woodland plants that flower in the spring: Hellebores (*Helleborus*), Snowdrops (*Galanthus*), Primroses (*Primula*), Bluebells (*Hyacinthoides*), *Pulmonaria* and Lily-of-the-Valley (*Convallaria*), for example. For early summer, Bleeding Hearts (*Dicentra*),

Leopard's Bane (*Doronicum*) and Foxgloves (*Digitalis*) are indispensable. Later come Day Lilies (*Hemerocallis*), Hostas, *Rodgersia* and the beautiful blue Himalayan Poppies (*Meconopsis*). The Welsh Poppy (*Meconopsis cambrica*) will provide colour throughout the summer. In the autumn *Kirengeshoma* creates interest, as do the delightful little *Cyclamen hederifolium*.

Many shrubs flower happily in shade, providing colour as well as permanent structure. Those with variegated foliage and evergreen foliage are particularly useful.

When should I start sowing annuals for the summer?

Hardy annuals can be sown in the autumn so that they flower early in the following season; they can also be sown outside in spring to flower later. At either time, they can be sown under glass in trays.

Half-hardy and tender annuals should be sown in the early spring under glass and not planted out until the threat of frost has passed. Do not sow them too early, as the seedlings may be ready for planting out long before time, and will become drawn and lose their vitality. Many of this group can also be sown directly in the soil after the frosts have passed.

▲ Sow tender and half-hardy annuals under glass, but not too early, as they will become drawn.

▲ Hardy annuals can be sown straight into the open ground in autumn or spring.

Some packets of seed say that the plants are half-hardy. What does this mean?

The term half-hardy is usually applied to annuals. It refers to the fact that the plants are susceptible to frost damage and should not be sown or planted outside before the threat of frost has receded. If germinated under glass in gentle heat, they should be sown six to eight weeks before they are due to be planted out.

The plants should be hardened off before planting out. This involves exposing them to outside temperatures for increasingly longer periods over the course of about two weeks. The best method is to put them in a cold frame and open it for longer amounts of time each day, eventually leaving it open at night as well.

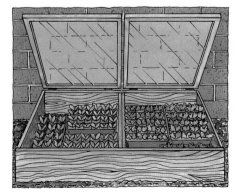

◄ Half-hardy and tender annuals need to be hardened off before they can be planted out in the garden. A cold frame is ideal.

There are unsightly orange spots on the leaves of my Hollyhocks. What are they and what can I do about them?

By choosing plants carefully, you can make a hot border look stunning all summer long.

▶ This is a fungal disease known as rust. It is a very common problem with Hollyhocks and one that is difficult to combat. It weakens the plant and makes it rather unsightly, but rarely causes too much damage and is likely to be a problem you and the Hollyhock can live with.

Although Hollyhocks are perennials, they can be treated as biennials and re-sown each year.

This ensures new plants which have a better chance of growing and flowering well before they are seriously attacked by rust. If you

Alcea rugosa is more resistant to rust than the normal garden Hollyhock.

▶

want to try and prevent the disease, burn all existing plants and plant new ones, raised from seed in fresh soil. Spray regularly with a fungicide, a mancozeb- or thiram-based product, as a deterrent. An alternative is to plant *Alcea rugosa*, a close relative of the normal garden Hollyhock (*Alcea rosea*) and one which is much more resistant to rust. The only disadvantage is that *Alcea rugosa* is only available with pale yellow flowers.

I like the idea of creating a border devoted to hot colours. Can you give me some idea of the plants I could use?

Hot borders provide excitement in the garden, but should not be overdone, as the eye can quickly become bored with them. The hot colours are those based on orange. Flaming reds and golden yellows are the other main ingredients. Avoid using reds that have a pink or purple tone in them, or yellows that have a hint of green. If possible, see the plants in flower before you buy them, to check that they are the right shades.

For the front of the border, there are several strong orange, red and brown Rock Roses (*Helianthemum*); two excellent golden Daisies in the form of *Inula ensifolia* and *Haplopappus*; and

Lychnis x *archwrightii*, which provides bright orange flowers against a rich purple foliage. Further back, you can try Red-hot Pokers (*Knifophia*) and *Helenium*. Montbretia (*Crocosmia*) also provides a wonderful range of oranges and flame reds, while Day Lilies (*Hemerocallis*) and Oriental Poppies (*Papaver orientalis*) come in a range of hot colours too.

For the back of the border, try some of the taller *Rudbeckia* or *Heliopsis* with striking, Daisy-like flowers. *Ligularia* 'The Rocket' will provide towering spires of gold, while Lilies provide bright orange and flame red flowers over a long period.

As a contrast to these flowers, use golden, purple or brown foliage, perhaps in the form of some of the variegated grasses and bamboos.

I live on the side of a windy hill and many of my herbaceous plants are blown over when in full flower. What is the best way of staking them?

There are several ways of staking plants, some more expensive than others. Always try to stake the plant before it has grown too high to provide support right from the beginning. One of the cheapest methods is to insert a number of canes around the plant and form a cat's cradle of string between them, through which the plant will grow and find support.

Another cheap method, if you have them available or could find some around the garden, is to use branched pea sticks. Again, place several around the outside of the plant, bend over the tops and tie them together, making a mesh of twigs which will support the stems of the plant as they grow up through it.

A similar, but more expensive, method is to buy special galvanised hoops which are supported on uprights and have crossing wires over the top. You can also buy proprietary wire stakes that link together around the plant providing support around the outside. These are especially useful for plants that have already collapsed and need to be strengthened. Although expensive, in the first place, metal supports will last for many years and can be used over and over again as required.

Individual stems of plants with tall, heavy flower spikes, such as Delphiniums, can be tied to canes or sticks with soft string or twine.

▲ Metal hoops offer strong support.

▲ Pea sticks provide discrete support.

▲ Sticks and string are inexpensive.

▲ Special metal stakes link together.

▲ Individual canes support tall spikes.

Some of my clumps of perennials have become dead and woody in the centre; when is the best time to divide them?

There are two methods of dividing herbaceous plants: one is to split them and put them straight back in the soil; the other is to make small divisions and pot them up in a cold frame or propagating case. For most plants, the latter method can be used at virtually any time during the growing season.

The former method, however, should not be carried out when the weather is very hot and dry. The best time is in the spring, when the soil is still moist and the weather reasonably mild, providing enough heat to allow the divisions to grow away. The autumn is also suitable, as long as the task is accomplished quite early and cold weather is not imminent. Otherwise the plants will sit in cold, wet soil until the spring before re-establishing

Do I need to put fertilizer on my flower borders? If so, what should I use?

Flowering plants, like all other plants, need food to put on growth and to survive. In nature, this is mainly provided by the decay of discarded leaves and dead plants. In the garden, however, we tend to tidy away all dead and dying matter, breaking the natural cycle. Therefore, it is vital to replenish the soil.

When a bed is first prepared, you should dig in as much organic material

growth, and they are likely to die.

Some perennials, such as the tap-rooted *Eryngium* and those with a single basal stem (*Erysimum* for example), cannot be divided.

▼ Lift old clumps of perennials in the spring, when the soil is not too wet.

▼ Divide each clump into individual pieces, discarding the woody centre.

▼ Replant after rejuvenating the soil with compost and humus, then water.

(compost, farmyard manure, leafmould, composted bark, etc) as possible. Once the bed has been planted, top-dress with more organic material in the autumn or spring. During the summer, particularly after a wet spring, it is a good idea to top-dress with a general fertilizer. Blood, fish and bone or bonemeal are ideal organic fertilisers, but a proprietary balanced inorganic fertilizer will be equally efficient. If you do not have access to sufficient organic matter, you should also top-dress with fertilizer in the spring.

▲ In the spring, top-dress the borders with well-rotted compost or shredded bark.

I am a flower arranger and would like to grow my own flowers for drying. What would you suggest?

The number of garden plants that can be dried is surprisingly large, and if you are a serious arranger it would be worth devoting a separate part of the garden to growing rows of such plants. However, if you only make the occasional arrangement, you could simply add selected plants to existing beds and borders.

The classic dried flowers are those that have papery bracts or petals, such as the *Helichrysum* and *Helipterum*. Another classic is Statice (*Limonium*). All may be grown purely for arranging, but regular border plants such as *Delphinium* (especially the double form), Honesty (*Lunaria*), Lavender (*Lavandula*), Bear's

Breeches (*Acanthus*), Masterwort (*Astrantia*) and the Sea Hollies (*Eryngium*) are also very good. Seedheads, such as those of the Poppies (*Papaver*), Love-in-a-mist (*Nigella*) and Onions (*Allium*) are excellent, while many grasses can also be effective when dried.

◀ The Sea Hollies (*Eryngium*) make excellent dried flowers, but beware - they are quite prickly.

The Winter-flowering Iris (*Iris unguicularis*) blooms from November to March. It thrives in a sunny spot, and prefers a soil that is not too rich.

I would like to have some plants in flower during the winter, especially at Christmas. What would you suggest?

In mild weather, it is surprising how many plants will continue to flower through the autumn and into winter. However, some plants are specifically winter flowerers.

Snowdrops (*Galanthus*) are a must. Hellebores (*Helleborus*) also provide a welcome splash of colour during the dull months; sadly, the Christmas Rose (*Helleborus niger*), despite its name, rarely flowers at Christmas, but waits for the New Year. The delightful yellow Winter Aconites (*Eranthis*) often accompany Snowdrops, while *Iris unguicularis* produces beautiful, scented flowers throughout the season. *Clematis cirrosa balearica* is a winter-flowering climber for a sheltered wall. The shrub *Lonicera fragrantissima* has the most delightful winter scent, and the Winter Boxes (*Sarcococca*) produce almost overpowering perfume.

A bright winter day is the ideal time to begin preparing for the following summer, but don't venture onto the borders if the soil is too wet.

When is the best time to tidy up a border: autumn or spring?

Strictly speaking, a border should be tidied constantly, removing old flower heads as they go over and taking out any weeds that appear. However, the main period of activity is usually restricted to either the autumn or spring. There are differing views on which is best.

In many respects, autumn is best because it means that most of the work is finished by the time that spring arrives, and the many jobs that need to be undertaken in spring can be carried out at a more leisurely pace. However, there are several arguments for leaving the work until the spring. For example the dead stems of plants can create an interesting picture during the winter. They also provide seed heads and a

▲ Remove all dead stems before the new growth becomes large enough to be damaged.

haven for insects, both of which are food for over-wintering birds. Finally, the canopy of dead stems will shelter a plant's crown, alleviating the worst of the frost.

I don't have much spare time for gardening, but I would like to grow a few perennials; can you tell me if this is possible?

Herbaceous borders are not as time consuming as is generally believed, and there is no reason why a person with limited time should not grow perennials. The secret is to choose plants that do not need staking or any attention, other than perhaps being cut to the ground in the autumn. There are many from which to choose, among them Purple Cone Flower (*Echinacea*), the low-growing Geraniums such as *Geranium sanguineum*, various Asters (including Michaelmas Daisies) and Pearl Everlasting (*Anaphalis*).

Mulching the borders with bark or spent mushroom compost will considerably reduce the amount of watering and weeding required. Stone or brick paths, rather than grass, adjacent to borders will save much time in cutting the edges and removing weeds that have spread from the grass.

◀ The expense of a mulch will be repaid by the time it saves in watering and weeding the borders.

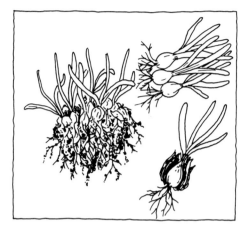

I have a large clump of Daffodils that have flowered well for many years, but this spring, despite producing masses of leaves, they have not flowered. Can you tell me why?

When dividing a large clump of Daffodil bulbs, tease the roots apart with your fingers, and remove the dry skins before replanting.

▶ The most likely problem with a large clump that has been in place for a long time is that the bulbs have become congested as new bulbs have formed alongside the old, impoverishing the soil as they fight for the limited supply of nourishment. Lift the whole clump, split it and replant the bulbs further apart in a fresh site.

You may be surprised at the number of bulbs you find, and you should be able to make several new clumps the size of your original. If you want to grow them on the same site, rejuvenate the soil before replanting by adding a low-nitrogen (N), high-potash (K) and high-phosphate (P) fertilizer.

My neighbour has some Cyclamen that flower in the garden in mid winter. I thought they were tender. What type could they be?

Most Cyclamen, especially the florist types, are tender and will not withstand a winter outside. However, a few species will grow happily

▲ A colourful mid winter display of *Cyclamen coum*.

outdoors. The example that you have seen is *Cyclamen coum*. This flowers around mid winter. Before this, in the autumn, *C. hederifolium* is in flower for a long period. During late winter and spring, *C. repandum* may be seen. Together, they will give many months of pleasure, especially as their leaves are also attractive.

All need the same conditions: a lightly-shaded position (under a deciduous tree or shrub perhaps) and a light soil that has been enriched with leafmould. No feeding is required, but a light top-dressing of leafmould each autumn will be beneficial. Avoid covering the leaves. They do best in bare soil, so remove all weeds.

TREES, SHRUBS & CLIMBERS

I recently replanted some Roses, but the new plants looked decidedly sick, so I replaced them with yet more and these also became sick. Why can't I grow Roses any more?

The trouble with your Roses is a familiar problem, but it is a problem that is not really understood. It is known as Replant Sickness or Rose Soil Sickness, and is caused by planting new Roses into soil from which old Roses have been removed. The old Roses may have been perfectly healthy, but they leave behind a legacy that prevents the new plants from establishing themselves.

There are only three ways of coping with the problem, none of which may be satisfactory from the gardener's point of view. The first option is to abandon the bed and dig a new bed elsewhere in the garden. The second is to remove all the soil that surrounded each original plant, digging a hole at least 2ft (60cm) square and 18in (45cm) deep, and replacing it with fresh soil. Obviously, this will be very hard work. The third course of action is to give up the idea of growing Roses for a few years.

▼ To ensure flourishing Roses, such as this 'Cornelia', never plant them in a bed that was previously used for other Roses.

What is the best shrub to use for a hedge?

For formal hedging, Yew (*Taxus*) is attractive and takes a lot of beating. It is slow growing and, therefore, only requires cutting once a year. Although other evergreen coniferous hedging plants are available, they are generally quick growing, needing regular cutting and attention to keep them neat.

Holly is also evergreen, but often discards prickly dead leaves in the borders, which can be a painful nuisance when weeding. It needs cutting once or twice a year. Privet

I have been told that it is dangerous to grow Ivy on a house wall. Is this true?

Ivy (*Hedera*) climbs by means of aerial roots that cling to their support. If a wall is sound, there should be no problems, as the roots will only grip the rough surface of the masonry. This applies to most modern walls.

On older buildings, however, especially those that have a soft lime mortar between the bricks or stones, the roots can

Although slow-growing, Box (*Buxus sempervirens*) is one of the most versatile hedging materials. It can be grown to any size or shape, and it will also tolerate regular clipping.

is quick growing, but consequently needs frequent cutting. It is semi-evergreen and can look scruffy as it ages. Hawthorn is deciduous and looks good in a rural setting. It needs cutting twice a year.

Beech and Hornbeam take a while to establish, but then both form a thick hedge which, although deciduous, retains its

dead, brown leaves throughout the winter. They need cutting twice a year. Box is very slow growing, but eventually makes a very dense hedge that only needs cutting once a year. It is ideal for small hedges. Loose-growing *Berberis* and *Rosa rugosa* make attractive informal hedges with only the occasional need for cutting.

penetrate and cause deterioration. Not only is the Ivy likely to enter the joints, but it can cause old bricks to crumble or flake if they are at all soft. In this case, the only solution is to remove the Ivy completely and use another climber that does not attach itself to the wall, but is dependent on trellising for its support.

Although Ivy is held in place by its aerial roots, these do not attempt to draw any nourishment from the wall.

▲ Ivy (*Hedera*) should not damage walls, as long as they are in sound condition.

I need to move a mature shrub. Is this possible and when should I attempt it?

To stand the best chance of being transplanted successfully, mature shrubs should be moved with care between mid autumn and early spring. Do this only when the weather and soil conditions are favourable.

First dig a trench around the plant, severing any roots as you go. Then dig under the plant, rolling it first one way, then the other so that you can place a large hessian sack or sheet of strong polythene under it. This will help keep the root-ball intact. The shrub can now be moved to its new site, which should be prepared thoroughly in readiness.

A mature shrub will be heavy, so enlist the aid of at least one other person when you move it. A strong stake can be tied horizontally to the base of the bush to act as a carrying handle.

▼ Left to right: To transplant a mature shrub, start by cutting around it with a sharp spade. Then dig a trench around it, and gradually slide sacking under it to hold the root-ball together. Strap a strong stake to the trunk to make a handle for lifting.

My *Cotinus* is leggy and sparse. Can I cut it back or will it die?

The young foliage of *Cotinus* (this example is *C. coggygria* 'Follis Purpureis') has the strongest colour, so prune regularly to maintain the young growth.

▶ *Cotinus* can be pruned heavily and shaped at any stage of its life. If left to develop, it will become a large bush, or even a tree. However, it is usually grown for its attractive foliage, which is always best when the shoots are cut back in spring to within two buds of the previous year's growth, creating a low, rounded bush. Although this technique does produce large, well-coloured leaves, a disadvantage is that flowers are rarely produced.

When flowers do appear, they are carried in large, airy clouds like puffs of smoke. They only grow on mature wood, so by removing the stems each year to obtain good foliage, you will lose

this feature. A compromise is to remove a third of the oldest stems each year, so that the bush will produce both attractive foliage and flowers. This principle can also be applied to many other shrubs: the Elders (*Sambucus*) for example.

▲ To maintain leaf colour without losing all the flowers on a *Cotinus*, prune back a third of the stems to within 3in (8cm) of ground level before growth starts in spring.

Shoots have arisen from the base of my 'Zéphirine Drouhin' Rose that have puzzled me. Unlike the thornless shoots of the main plant, these have thorns. Why is this?

Many Roses are grafted onto a Dog Rose (*Rosa canina*) rootstock. These frequently throw up stems ('suckers') from below the graft, especially if they have been damaged below ground by a fork or spade while the bed was being tended. These suckers are pure Dog Rose and will produce both the thorns and flowers of this vigorous hedgerow plant. In the worst case, it will take over completely from the grafted Rose.

Suckers should be removed, preferably by pulling them from

Can I mix trees and shrubs with herbaceous plants in the same border?

In times gone by, plants were often segregated by their type, particularly in large gardens with plenty of space. Nowadays, with gardens generally being smaller, the mixed border has become a firm favourite.

One major advantage of mixing plants is that a permanent structure of trees and shrubs can be created to provide interest throughout the year, while herbaceous plants add colour and vitality during the warmer, sunnier seasons. Thus a continually changing scene can be created, which is more difficult to achieve with trees and shrubs alone. A further advantage is that

shrubs can look dull between flowering and producing autumn colour. Herbaceous plants in front of, or around them will not only fill gaps, but also divert the eye when a shrub or tree is at its least interesting.

▲ Mixing shrubs and perennials will increase the colours and textures available, as well as provide the border with structure all year round. This is particularly important during the winter.

the rootstock. Failing this, cut them back as tightly as possible to the underground stem. Do not cut them off at ground level, as this promotes more growth, usually in the form of several stems instead of the original single stem. Any other suckers should be removed

as soon as they appear.

If you still have problems, replant with a new 'Zéphirine Drouhin' that has been grafted onto a new sucker-free rootstock, such as *Rosa* 'Laxa'. This applies to any grafted Rose, not just 'Zéphirine Drouhin'.

◀ Always remove suckers as soon as they are seen. Scrape away the soil and trace the sucker back to the root from which it rises. Then carefully tear or cut it away as close to its source as possible.

How do I go about pruning my trees and shrubs?

Top: Prune stems just above a pair of opposing strong shoots or buds. Centre: If shoots or buds are staggered, choose a strong one and prune just above it. Bottom: Make cuts at an angle, from a point level with the base of the bud to a point just above the top.

When removing a branch from a tree, the initial cut should be an undercut some distance from the trunk. This will prevent the weight from splitting the branch down to, and into, the trunk. Then a second cut can be made slightly further out, severing the branch. A final cut is made close to the trunk, removing the resulting snag.

▶ Pruning woody plants can seem rather daunting, but you will soon find that it is not as frightening as it first seemed. It is essential to make clean cuts, so always use good-quality, sharp secateurs and saws. The cut should be close to a bud, to a joint in the branch, or to the trunk; never leave a 'snag'. The pruning cut should be just above a viable bud and angled backwards at about 30 degrees.

▼ The first thing to do is remove any dead wood. Then cut out any wood that crosses over or rubs against any other branches, at the same time generally shaping the tree or bush. For some, this is sufficient, but many shrubs need up to a third of the old wood removed to promote the growth of vigorous new material from the base. In some cases, many of the Butterfly Bushes (*Buddleja*) for example, shrubs need to be cut to the ground each year. Consult a reliable reference source for the exact treatment of individual trees and shrubs.

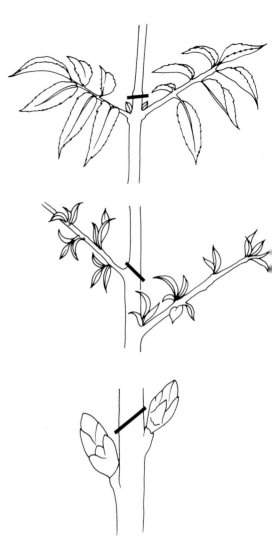

I only have a small town garden, but would like to grow some trees. Which do you recommend?

It is easy to become carried away when you see young trees in a garden centre, forgetting the ultimate size they will achieve. A Weeping Willow (*Salix babylonica*), for example, is a very bad choice, as not only will its canopy rapidly fill a small garden, but its roots will do likewise, making it impossible to grow anything under it. Some trees, however, never grow too large.

Among the most decorative of small trees are some of the Maples (*Acer*), but avoid the Sycamore (*A. pseudoplatanus*). The Mountain Ashes (*Sorbus*) are a wonderful group of trees for small gardens, as are several of the Crab Apples (*Malus*). Many of the Ornamental

Flowering Cherries, such as this *Prunus* 'Shirotae', make the most delightful trees for town gardens, providing stunning flowers in spring and dappled shade in summer.

Cherries (*Prunus*) remain small enough and are particularly eye-catching in spring. There are some very attractive Hawthorns (*Crataegus*) that are worth considering, especially for their autumn colour. The Silver Weeping Pear (*Pyrus salicifolia* 'Pendula') remains one of the most popular trees for small gardens.

I like variegated shrubs and trees, but I have never seen a whole border of them. Is there any reason why I should not create one?

The wonderful aspect of variegated foliage is that the mixture of colour creates a vibrant image. However, if there are too many variegated plants in a border, it will look very 'busy', and the enjoyment will be lost.

Such plants are best mixed with plain-leaved varieties. If you have the opportunity to visit other people's gardens, note which shrubs associate best with your favourite variegated plants. Then gradually build up a sympathetic

picture that enables you to have the maximum number of variegated plants without the border becoming visually uncomfortable.

Mixing variegated shrubs needs to be done with much care and thought, as in this case. Otherwise they will create a restless atmosphere.

I am thinking of planting a tree. Do I need to stake it and, if so, what is the best method?

Except in very well protected areas, it is always best to stake a newly-planted tree. Even in protected areas, the practice has a lot to recommend it.

At one time it was thought that a tree had to be staked for the full length of its trunk, but modern practice is to stake only the base. This prevents the roots from moving, but allows the trunk and branches to sway, thus toughening them and helping them resist damage from the wind. If the base moves, the root-ball tends to rock, severing any new roots attempting to push out into the soil. This will not only stunt the tree's growth, but also affect its stability.

Place a short stake in the ground before the tree is planted (if you do it afterwards, you may sever unseen roots), and secure the trunk to it with a proprietary tree tie. This should be slackened gradually over the next few years as the trunk expands, until eventually it can be removed.

Using proper tree ties, secure the trunk of the tree to a low, firm stake. This will prevent the base of the tree from moving in the soil. If necessary, use two ties, 18in (45cm) apart.

What is the best method of attaching a climber to a wall?

An old method of fixing a climber to a wall was to use nails with lead tags. These were hammered into the wall along the line of the stems and bent over them. When the plant was pruned, the nails and tags were removed, and a new set hammered in for the new stems. Unfortunately, this technique has little to recommend it, as eventually it tends to ruin the wall.

A better method of supporting a climber is to fix a wooden trellis, or a stiff plastic or metal mesh, to

When is the best time to prune my shrubs?

Removal of dead wood and cosmetic pruning can usually be carried out at any time. However, the timing of the main pruning effort can be critical, as it will affect the following season's flowering.

If the shrubs flower on mature wood, as *Deutzia* does, they should be pruned immediately after flowering so that the new wood has a chance to grow and mature before the next flowering season. If cut in the winter, the new growth will be too young to produce flowers. Many other plants produce flowers on new wood and can be pruned in the winter or spring, Fuchsias for example.

Consult a reliable reference work to discover when each

the wall. Attach this with the aid of wooden spacers so that it is held at least 1in (2.5cm) away from the surface. A wooden trellis can be fixed in such a way that it is hinged along its bottom edge, allowing the climber to be eased away from the wall for painting or renovation.

An alternative is to drive vine eyes into the wall and stretch horizontal wires through them. Use a tensioning screw at one end to keep each wire taut.

Some climbers, such as Ivies (*Hedera*) and *Hydrangea anomala petiolaris*, are self-clinging and need no support.

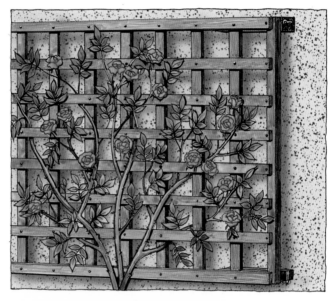

▲ Wooden trellising, spaced about 1in (2.5cm) from the wall, makes an ideal support. If, as here, the bottom is hinged and the top hooked, the trellis plus the climber can be eased away to allow access to the wall for painting or other maintenance.

shrub needs pruning, or work it out for yourself by noting the type of wood on which the flowers are produced. A few shrubs are grown for the decorative effect of their coloured stems in winter: *Salix alba* 'Britzensis' and *Rubus cockburnianus* for

▲ The coloured stems of *Salix alba* 'Britzensis' glow in the winter sunshine.

example. The coloration tends to be strongest on the newer wood, so these shrubs should be pruned hard in the spring to produce new growth for the following winter.

Is it advisable to grow climbers through trees?

A rambling Rose cascading from an ancient, but healthy, Apple tree. Once established, such a Rose needs little care and attention.

► This is a difficult question to answer, as so much depends on the condition of the tree. If it is healthy and sound, there should be no problem. If the tree is dead or dying, the additional burden of a climber, especially in a strong wind, may bring the whole lot crashing down. Having said that, the dead stumps of trees can make excellent climbing frames for plants, as long as they are not too tall or too rotten.

Clematis, especially the varieties of *C. montana* and high-growing species such as *C. rehderiana*, are ideal for growing through trees. Climbing and rambling Roses are also splendid plants, many growing to an incredible height. Sweet-smelling cultivars and species are particularly worthwhile. *Rosa* 'Félicité Perpétué', 'Bobbie James' and 'Rambling Rector' are but three of the many that are suitable.

Russian Vine (*Fallopa baldschuanica*) is often seen scrambling through trees. This has the advantage of being late-flowering, but it can really smother a tree, sometimes weakening it.

Attractive bark is always eye-catching. This *Prunus serrula* displays a coppery sheen that glows beautifully in the evening sun.

I would like to buy a tree with a decorative bark. Which are the best varieties?

Attractive bark adds yet another dimension to the decorative qualities of a tree, especially in winter when many trees have lost their leaves, exposing the trunks and lower branches.

Some bark is attractive simply because of the cracks and fissures it contains: mature Oaks (*Quercus*) and Sweet Chestnut (*Castanea*), for example, display these features. On the other hand,

Can you tell me the best time to prune Clematis?

There is no simple answer to this question, as Clematis vary in their needs. They are divided into three groups, each treated differently.

Group One consists of the vigorous growers, such as *C. montana*. Other than having dead wood cut out and being kept tidy, they need no attention. Since they flower on the previous season's wood, pruning should be carried out immediately after flowering.

Group Two comprises the large-flowered varieties, the blooms being produced on stems arising from last year's wood. Cut out dead wood and prune weak growth to a good pair of buds in the early spring before growth starts.

Group Three covers plants that flower on new wood. Cut back hard in the early spring, to a good pair of buds, usually 12-24in (30-60cm) from the ground. Most books and catalogues devoted to Clematis specify each plant's group.

some barks are coloured, such as the white papery examples of the Birch (*Betula*), especially *B. utilis jacquemontii*. Some Birches, such as *B. ermanii*, have a warmer, pinkish-brown bark.

The best of the brown barks are the shiny, copper-coloured variety of *Prunus serrula* and the peeling, papery bark of *Acer griseum*. Yet another group, known as the Snake Barked Maples, have decorative white veins set off against green or purple stems. Among these are *Acer davidii* and *A. pensylvanicum*.

▲ Group One Clematis need little pruning other than the removal of dead wood. However, if too rampant, they may be cut back after flowering.

▲ Group Two Clematis should have dead wood removed in spring, after which the remaining shoots can be cut back to a good pair of shoots.

▲ Group Three Clematis need heavy pruning. In early spring, cut back each shoot to a strong pair of buds, 12-24in (30-60cm) from the ground.

My golden variegated *Eleagnus* has branches of pure green leaves. What has gone wrong and what should I do about it?

Shrubs with variegated leaves are abnormal forms of green-leaved plants. These abnormalities often occur as a 'sport', where one of the shoots on an otherwise normal plant appears variegated. The keen-eyed gardener may spot this, remove the shoot, and use it as a cutting to propagate a new plant that is entirely variegated.

Many variegated shrubs produce shoots that revert to the original green colour of the parent. These shoots should be removed, as they will take over the whole plant.

Most variegated plants are quite stable; that is they continue to be variegated and produce variegated offsprings from cuttings. Occasionally, however, stems 'revert', producing leaves in the plant's original unvariegated coloration. These reversions are quite vigorous and, unless they are removed, may eventually become the major part of the plant, the variegated parts dying out. The remedy is simple: as soon as you see a green shoot on a variegated plant, cut it out.

When buying trees and shrubs, I have often seen them described as specimen plants. Can you tell me what this means?

Some plants, trees and shrubs have such strong personalities that they are best seen in isolation; their shape, or flower or leaf qualities may be lost if mixed with other plants or planted in a group. In the right setting, a single specimen is all that is required. A specimen plant tends to draw the eye, so it is perfect for use as a focal point at the end of a path, or in an expanse of grass, possibly at the far end of a lawn.

Site specimen plants so that they can be seen from several directions. They can be kept in containers and placed on patios, or even moved about the garden as the scene changes with the seasons.

▲ The beautiful *Rhododendron* 'Beau Belles' makes a fine specimen in a tub.

VEGETABLES

What type of soil do you need to be able to grow vegetables successfully?

While some types of soil are better than others, very few are totally unsuitable for growing vegetables. Anyone who wishes to grow their own vegetables should be able to do so.

The ideal soil is a rich loam, that is free-draining, but at the same time moisture-retentive. This means that excess water drains away, but sufficient is left behind for the plants' needs. It should be workable even after a cloudburst. The texture should be crumbly, without being too fine or too solid. This allows both air and water to reach the roots, both being essential for good growth. The soil should also be slightly acid: pH6-6.5 is ideal for most vegetables.

Very few of us have soil that combines all these qualities, but after several years of digging-in organic material, even the most stubborn soil can be made to yield good results. Well-rotted farmyard manure, garden compost or any other suitable organic matter will help to break down clay soils, and make sandy soils more moisture-retentive and richer in nutrients.

▼ A well-tended vegetable garden is as much a delight to the eye as it is to the palate. Most gardens can be coaxed into producing at least some vegetables.

Why do my Tomatoes split as they ripen?

The problem is that you have not watered them regularly. If the developing Tomato is allowed to dry out, the skin starts to toughen, and when growth begins again as water becomes available, the skin splits as the Tomato expands. Regular watering, whether the plants are outside or in a greenhouse, is the solution.

▲ Split Tomatoes result from irregular watering.

Radishes, like these ▶ examples of 'Pink Beauty', may split if they are allowed to dry out.

Radishes will not ▶ swell if the plants are overcrowded. Thin out the seedlings as early as possible.

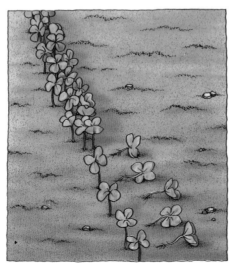

Only a few of my Radishes have filled out. I thought they were supposed to be foolproof; what am I doing wrong?

Radishes are easy to grow as long as you remember two points: they must not be overcrowded, and they must not go short of water. Sow them very thinly in the row, and if they come up in groups or patches, thin them as soon as you can. Water the ground before you sow, and keep it watered during any dry spells. They must not be inundated with water, just moist; any dry spell will check their growth and cause them to split when they receive water again.

Radishes can be sown thinly in seed rows of slow-germinating vegetables, such as Parsnips. This not only utilises the ground between the groups of station-sown seeds (at 8in/20cm intervals), but also quickly marks the row so that it is possible to hoe or weed along it without disturbing the Parsnips before they appear above ground.

Can you tell me what is meant by intercropping?

The purpose of intercropping is to obtain the maximum amount of produce from a given piece of ground. This is not so crucial in a large garden, but where space is limited, it makes sound sense.

Intercropping takes advantage of the fact that some crops grow faster than others. Radishes, for example, can be sown in the same row as Parsnips, because the latter will have hardly grown before the former are harvested.

Other crops can similarly be mixed. Lettuces are useful for intercropping. Plant a row of them close to young Tomato plants, and they will be eaten long before the Tomatoes require their space. Similarly, they can be planted between young Brassicas.

My young Cabbage plants are always ruined by birds before they have a chance to grow. How can I protect them?

There are many traditional methods of scaring away birds, but unfortunately most of them fail to work. Hanging old polythene bags or streamers of silver foil have little effect, other than to make the garden look messy. Even modern whistling tapes seem to have little effect, except that if set close enough together they make it difficult for the birds to land.

The most effective method is to net the Cabbages. This will exclude the birds completely. As a bonus, if you use a tight-weave net or fleece, butterflies cannot reach the Cabbages to lay their eggs, so you will have caterpillar-free plants as well.

◀ The best way to protect Cabbage seedlings from bird damage is to cover them with fine netting, supported by twigs and anchored at the edges by stones.

My garden is not big enough for a vegetable plot, but can I grow vegetables in containers?

A wide range of containers can be used for growing vegetables. The best, although not very pretty, are growing bags. These are filled with specially formulated compost.

▶ Vegetables are no different from other plants, except that we eat them, so they can be grown in containers in the same way. You can use tubs, pots or special polythene growing bags containing a formulated compost.

Containers dry out very quickly, so it is very important to water at least once a day, and more frequently in hot weather. This constant watering washes the nutrients from the soil, so a liquid feed should be regularly added to the water (as directed on the packaging). Nearly every type of

vegetable can be grown in this way, but quick-growing (Lettuces for example) or productive plants (such as Tomatoes) are best.

Is there any advantage in buying strips of vegetable ▼ seedlings from a garden centre compared to raising my own?

When buying seedlings from garden centres, choose those that are well spaced in their trays or, as here, in separate cells. Avoid overcrowded, drawn seedlings.

The main advantage of buying seedlings is that it is very convenient, saving the considerable time and space needed to grow your own. This is particularly important if you don't possess a greenhouse or cold frame. It also removes the need to buy and store seed compost, seed trays and pots.

However, there are many advantages to growing your own plants from seed. In the first place, they are cheaper: you will get more for your money. Secondly, you will enjoy a much larger choice of varieties. Nurseries usually offer only one or, at best, two varieties of each type of vegetable, whereas a seed catalogue may list a dozen or more, all offering slight variations in taste and season.

A third reason is that strips of seedlings are often overcrowded. The plants may be drawn and spindly, and the roots restricted and tangled. If you can manage to do so, it is definitely preferable to grow your own from seed.

Is it possible to freeze any of the vegetables I grow?

There are times when the garden produces more vegetables than can be consumed. Although the excess can be given away, there still may be waste, so it is sensible to store as much as possible for times when the supply of fresh produce is limited.

Most vegetables can be frozen, but although they retain their flavour, many lose their firmness. Courgettes (Zucchini), for example, become rather soft, and while they can be used in casseroles and tarts, normally they are not crisp enough to be used on their own.

Peas and Beans of all types are

Turnips, Carrots and Potatoes - should be stored in a frost-free shed for much of the winter. Some, such as Carrots and Parsnips, can be frozen when they are young, but most are best cooked and

▲ Courgettes are often produced in such quantities that they cannot be consumed quickly enough. Freeze the excess for use later.

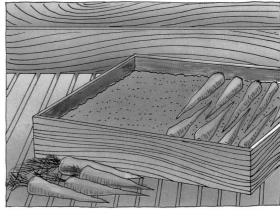

some of the most rewarding vegetables to freeze, as they retain their shape and flavour. They are often produced in large quantities and can be grown specifically for freezing. Onions, however, do not freeze well and should be stored in a dry, airy place away from frost. Most herbs can be frozen.

Some vegetables are best left in the ground or stored in a shed. Rootcrops - Parsnips, Beetroot,

puréed if you want to freeze them.

Seed strains are often available that have been especially selected because of the resulting vegetables' suitability for freezing. Most seed catalogues indicate those that are best for this treatment. With the exception of Sweet Peppers, most vegetables benefit from being blanched before they are frozen. This involves boiling them briefly, then cooling them rapidly.

▲ Onions (left) look attractive when stored in 'ropes'. Choose a dry, frost-free place. Carrots (right) can be stored in boxes of sand or peat.

Can you tell me why it is necessary to practise crop rotation?

If the same crop is grown repeatedly on the same soil, it not only depletes the soil of certain nutrients, but also increases the risk of a concentration of pests relevant to that crop. However, if crops are moved from one patch of soil to another each year, both problems are reduced, improving the quality and quantity of the yields with no expense involved.

The basic idea is to divide the vegetable garden into four separate plots: three for rotation, and the fourth for permanent crops such as Rhubarb and Globe Artichokes. In the first year, bed one contains the root crops plus the Onions, bed two contains the Brassicas (Cabbage, Cauliflower, etc), while bed three contains the Peas and Beans, Lettuce, Spinach and Chards. In the second year, the Peas, etc are moved to bed one, the root crops to bed two, and the Brassicas to bed three. In the third year, everything is moved on again, and so on.

▲ Vegetables and herbs planted in decorative beds, giving the overflowing effect of a small cottage garden.

◀ A more controlled version of a potager. Although this creates a delightfully serene picture, it is a productive garden.

What is a potager?

A potager is a vegetable garden that has been laid out to be decorative as well as productive. It usually consists of a number of beds separated by brick or gravel paths, and sometimes edged by Box or similar hedges. Often a symmetrical design will be used, but this can be difficult to maintain if the vegetables are to be eaten. The beds can be laid out in quite complex patterns, as in a knot garden.

Vegetables are often decorative in their own right. Runner Beans, for example, are very attractive, and Tomatoes were used for decoration long before anyone thought to eat them. You can take advantage of such plants by planting them in flower borders and beds, or by growing them in containers on patios.

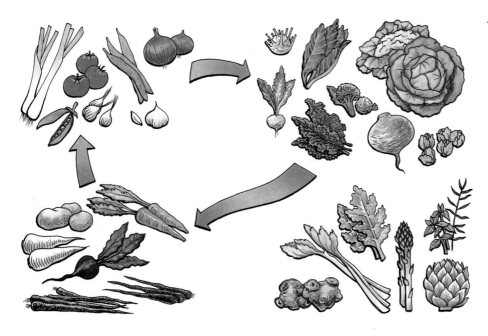

By dividing the vegetable garden into four areas, and rotating the contents of three of them annually, you will make the garden more productive and less prone to disease.

I am finding it difficult to obtain pea sticks (pea stakes). Can you recommend any alternatives?

The advantage of using pea sticks is that they are usually free and they come from a renewable source (Hazel is one of the best). However, they are becoming difficult to obtain. The simplest solution is to grow a short variety of Pea, which either needs no support or can be supported by a length of string stretched along each side of the row. For taller varieties, plastic netting can be stretched between posts.

A more permanent solution is to use wire netting, which will last for years. It can either be left outside during the winter, or rolled up and stored under cover.

Traditionally, peas are grown up pea sticks cut from the hedgerows.

Dwarf varieties need only parallel strings to support them.

Tall varieties can be grown through plastic or wire netting.

Can I grow herbs in my vegetable garden, or is it best to have a separate herb garden?

The herbs will not be affected by where they are grown, so it really depends on your preference. Although a herb garden can be an attractive feature, it will need a lot of maintenance.

Herbs will grow anywhere. Here they are combined with ornamental plants in an old-fashioned potager.

Well-prepared soil produces an abundant crop of vegetables. On poor soils, especially those that lose their nutrients through leeching, it may be necessary to feed with fertilizers during the growing season.

One of the best ways is to grow the most frequently used herbs (Mint and Parsley for example) close to the kitchen door. This may be in a vegetable plot if it happens to be nearest, or even in a flower border. An alternative is to use a herb pot, but this will require constant watering. If there is no space near the door, try to plant them near a path so that they can be harvested easily.

The herbs that are used less frequently can be grown further away, perhaps in part of the vegetable garden. Few take up much space, so they can be used to fill odd spaces, while shrubby varieties that need a permanent site, such as Rosemary and Sage, can be grown in flower borders.

I've prepared the soil with plenty of manure, but do I need to feed my vegetables once planted or sown?

Digging-in farmyard manure or compost will help provide the soil with a good structure, and increase its fertility and moisture-retaining capacity. In a soil that has been treated in this way over a number of seasons, the fertility should be sufficient to last from one year to the next, and normally no extra feeding will be required.

In poor soils, however, or where there is leeching (washing out of nutrients) by heavy rainfall or constant watering, the nutrients will need replacing at regular intervals. The easiest way to do this during the growing season is to top-dress with fertilizer. Test the soil first, using one of the many kits available, then apply

the appropriate fertilizer to rejuvenate the soil. Alternatively, you could do as many other gardeners: use a general-purpose fertilizer, such as organic bonemeal or a proprietary inorganic brand, following the manufacturer's instructions.

I would like to grow Chicory, but is it difficult to blanch?

You can eat Chicory green, but the leaves taste bitter. For a sweeter flavour, it is essential to force and blanch the leaves, ideally indoors.

Grow the plants outside, then just before the onset of winter cut off the leaves ½-1in (1-2.5cm) above the crown. Store these in a cool place in moist peat (or peat substitute) or sand. At intervals during winter, plant a few roots in a deep box of peat, covering them to a depth of about 10in (25cm).

Alternatively, plant them in deep pots and cover with a lightproof container. Move the pots into the warm (10-18°C/50-64°F) to initiate growth. After 3-5 weeks, they should be ready for harvesting.

◄ When dealing with fertilizers, always follow the manufacturer's recommendations, particularly with regard to safety and quantities.

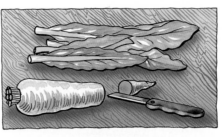

◄ Remove the leafy crown of each plant and, if necessary, trim back the root.

◄ Plant upright in a pot of peaty compost, the crowns level with the surface. Keep just moist.

◄ After 3-5 weeks in a warm, dark place, the leaves should be large enough for harvesting.

What is the best method of sowing vegetable seed?

This very much depends on the vegetables concerned. Most are best sown directly into the soil, normally in shallow drills. Prepare a seed bed, breaking the soil into a fine tilth. Then, using a string line for guidance, draw out a shallow groove (drill) with the corner of a hoe or a pointed stick. Sow the seed thinly along this. Mark and label the row, then cover with a thin layer of soil. Water using a can fitted with a fine rose.

Another method is to grow vegetables in blocks. In this case, the seed is evenly broadcast over the prepared bed and gently raked in. Then it is watered.

Some seed (Celery and Tomatoes, for example) must be started off in gentle heat in a greenhouse, or on a kitchen

▲ Indoor seed should be sown well spaced in trays or pots. Cover with a thin layer of compost.

window sill. Although they will grow if sown outside, they will be so late that they will not crop. These should be sown in a good sowing compost and kept moist in a propagator or polythene bag until they have germinated. Prick out, harden off and plant out. The packet should tell you whether to sow seeds outside or under glass.

▲ Draw out a row with the corner of a hoe, using string as a guide.

▲ Sow the seed thinly so that little thinning out of the seedlings will be necessary.

▲ Gently draw the soil back over the seed, filling in the drill completely.

▲ Firm the soil gently, then water using a can fitted with a fine rose.

▲ Keep the seed enclosed in a propagator or polythene bag until ready to be pricked out.

▲ Prick out the seedlings into individual pots and return to a propagator or cold frame.

When is the best time to thin seedlings?

It is important to sow seed thinly, which removes a lot of the necessity for thinning. Normally, however, it is necessary to remove at least a few seedlings to give the others room to grow. This should be done as early as possible, so that the roots of the remaining seedlings are not disturbed. When the seedlings are large enough to handle, pull out the excess, thinning to the recommended distances. Then water the row to settle any disturbed earth around the remaining plants.

Plants that need to be some distance apart, Parsnips for example, should be station sown to reduce the amount of thinning needed. Groups of three seeds are sown with the recommended spacing between the groups. Remove two of the seedlings at each station if they all germinate.

◀ Thin rows of seedlings so that the remaining plants have room to develop fully.

◀ Those that need a wider spacing can be station sown. Seed is sown in groups of three at the eventual growing distance.

◀ Once the seedlings develop, the surplus is removed, leaving one plant in each position.

Traditionally, vegetables are grown in rows. Space should be left between them to allow access for weeding and harvesting.

▲ How much space should I leave between rows of different vegetables?

In recent years there has been much interest in adopting the old-fashioned method of growing vegetables in blocks, but the majority of gardeners still seem to prefer growing them in rows. Basically, the spacing should allow the plants to grow without smothering each other, and also provide the gardener with room to tend and collect the crop.

The following is a selection of ideal planting distances:

Asparagus 36in (90cm)
Aubergines 18in (45cm)
Beetroot 12in (30cm)
Broad Beans 24in (60cm)
Cardoons 24in (60cm)
Carrots 6in (15cm)
Celeriac 15in (38cm)
Celery 24in (60cm)
Chicory 12in (30cm)
Courgettes (Zucchini) 36in (90cm)
Cucumbers 36in (90cm)
Endive 12in (30cm)
Florence Fennel 18in (45cm)
French Beans 18in (45cm)
Globe Artichokes 36in (90cm)
Jerusalem Artichokes 36in (90cm)
Kohlrabi 10in (25cm)
Lettuce 12in (30cm)
Marrows 36in (90cm)
Parsnips 12in (30cm)
Peas 24in (60cm)
Peppers 18in (45cm)
Potatoes 24in (60cm)
Pumpkins 36in (90cm)
Radishes 6in (15cm)
Rhubarb 36in (90cm)
Runner Beans 36in (90cm)
Salsify 12in (30cm)
Scorzonera 12in (30cm)
Swedes 15in (38cm)
Sweet Corn 24in (60cm)
Tomatoes 30in (80cm)
Turnips 10in (25cm)

FRUIT

Would the pollination requirements of some fruits prevent them from being grown on a small scale?

Many types of tree fruit (Apples, Cherries, Pears and Plums) are not self-fertile and need another variety to pollinate them. If you are lucky, your neighbours' gardens will meet this need, but if there are no other fruit trees in the immediate neighbourhood, you will have to grow at least two different varieties. What you choose does not matter, as long as the blossom appears at the same time. Most specialist catalogues and nurseries will help you choose compatible varieties.

A few varieties, particularly Plums, and increasingly Cherries, are self-fertile, so they can be grown on their own. Bush and soft fruit do not seem to suffer from the same problem.

▼ A fan-trained Morello cherry. This cooking Cherry is self-fertile and does not need a companion to produce fruit.

A well-supported row of new Raspberry canes, each being tied into a permanent wired structure. ▶

Is there any way I can grow Grapes outdoors?

To a certain extent, the answer must depend on where you live. You should have no problem if you live in a warm, temperate climate and enjoy long, hot summers. However, there are varieties that can be grown in much cooler areas. Unfortunately, they are not likely to produce high-quality dessert Grapes, but will provide plenty of smaller, succulent fruit that

Can you tell me how to prune and train Raspberries?

Raspberries are not difficult to cope with. In fact, they are among the easiest of fruits to prune.

For summer-fruiting varieties, remove all the old canes at ground level as soon as they have fruited. Tie in the new canes - which are usually a fresh green, as opposed to the brown of the old canes - to their supports. Continue to tie in

as the canes grow. In late winter, when these canes come back into growth, cut back the tip of each to a good bud just above the top wire of the supports.

For autumn-fruiting varieties, remove the canes in late winter. In both cases, the supports should comprise three parallel wires set about 30in (75cm), 42in (1.1m) and 60in (1.5m) above the ground. They should be stretched between well-braced posts.

▼ After fruiting cut off the old Raspberry canes cleanly at the base.

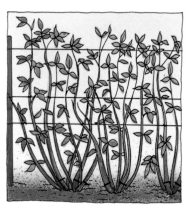

▼ Tie in the new canes to the wire framework, spacing them evenly.

▼ In late winter, when the canes start into growth, remove the tip of each.

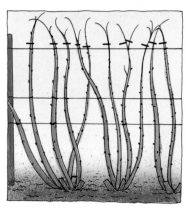

can be eaten or used for making wine.

In cool areas, choose a sheltered site, ideally backed by a wall. A local garden centre will help with varieties most likely to succeed in your area, but generally 'Brant' is a good dessert variety, while 'Triomphe d'Alsace' makes a good red wine, and 'Müller Thurgau' a good white. One major problem is from birds, which can only be overcome by covering the vines with netting as the fruit ripens.

There are several Apple trees in my new garden that produce lots of fruit. How can I store the excess for the winter?

Apples from the shops in winter have been kept in cold stores that maintain them in prime condition. You can store them at home without this facility, but the result may not always be so perfect.

Some Apples store better than others: Worcester Pearmain, for example, do not store at all, while Cox's will last well into spring. Some only have a limited storage life: Blenheims Orange are superb at Christmas, but go off after that.

Only choose unblemished fruit to store. The best method is to wrap each Apple in greaseproof paper and place them in trays. Put these in a cool, dark, frost-free place where the air is not too dry. You can also freeze Apples if they have been sliced or pre-cooked.

▲ Apple trees not only act as structural elements in the garden design, but they are also productive, often embarrassingly so. With care, however, the fruit can be stored to provide pleasure during the winter.

▼ Wrap each Apple in a sheet of paper; greaseproof is best.

▼ Place single layers of Apples in trays. Store in a cool, frost-free place.

▼ Small quantities can be kept in plastic bags. Keep a check for rotten fruit.

▲ The first task is to remove all dead, dying or damaged branches.

▲ Then cut out any branches that cross or rub against their neighbours.

▲ Finally, if the fruiting spurs are overcrowded, thin them out.

I have taken over a garden with some neglected Apple trees. How can I restore them?

A restored tree will not only look much tidier, but also crop better. First remove any dead, dying or diseased wood. Then cut out any overcrowded branches, or any that rub or cross other branches. The tree should now be more open.

To open the tree further, remove any central growth so that sunlight can reach the crown. Also cut out any long branches that cannot easily be reached from the ground or a secure ladder. Cut some of the lower branches back by about a third to encourage new side shoots. Finally, thin the fruiting spurs if overcrowded.

If all of these treatments are necessary, they may be too much of a shock to the tree's system if done together, so spread the work over two or three years. Once the tree has been renovated, continue with a regular annual prune.

▲ Fresh fruit from the garden, such as these Redcurrants, is unbeatable.

So much fruit is available in the shops all year, that is it really worth growing?

Fruit can take up a great deal of space and needs a lot of attention: keeping pests and diseases at bay, constant pruning, and so on. All in all, there does not seem to be much to recommend growing it. However, once you have tasted fresh fruit direct from the plant you won't want to

I have a solid, south-facing fence and would like to grow Peaches against it. How do I fan-train them?

Fan-training allows the fruit to receive the maximum sunlight for ripening, yet reduces the space required. To support the branches, attach horizontal wires to the fence, about 6in (15cm) apart.

In the autumn, plant a maiden or two-year-old tree that has been prepared as a fan. Then, in the spring, choose two strong laterals about 12in (30cm) from the ground and angled at 40-45 degrees. Prune them to 15-18in (38-45cm), removing any laterals below them.

In summer select four shoots on each branch: one as the leader or continuation of the main branch, two on the upper side, and one below. Tie these into angled canes and remove all other shoots. In the winter cut back each shoot to a good bud, about 20-24in (50-60cm) from the base of last year's growth. Continue in this way until a fan-like structure fills the fence.

go back to the shop.

One major advantage of growing your own fruit is the vast range of varieties. To save space, trees and shrubs can be cordoned or fan-trained against fences, which is not only a practical solution, but also a decorative one. By carefully choosing varieties, you can ensure a long season, and can freeze or bottle surplus to provide for the barren months.

▲ After planting, cut back to two main lateral branches.

▲ In summer, remove all but four main shoots on each side and tie in.

▲ Continue to expand the fan shape, removing all superfluous shoots.

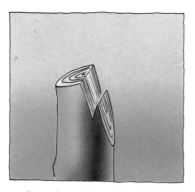

▲ Cut and notch the rootstock, shaping the tip at an angle if the scion is thin.

▲ Make a similar cut in the scion so that the two fit closely together.

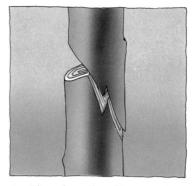

▲ Join, sealing with grafting wax or tape. The angled tip allows water to run off.

How can I create a standard Gooseberry bush?

This is quite a lengthy process, unless you buy a plant already trained. To do it yourself, you must be able to graft.

Root a cutting of either *Ribes odoratum* or *R. divaricatum* and grow it on as a single vertical stem. Reduce all side shoots to a few buds, leaving just enough to produce food for the plant's growth. After its third year, remove these side shoots and graft onto the stem the variety of Gooseberry you wish to grow.

The most common grafting technique for fruit trees is whip-and-tongue, but use another if you are more familiar with it. The Gooseberry should become established during the following summer. It can be pruned and trained during subsequent winters as you would a ground-level bush.

I have a small town garden and want to grow a few Apple trees. What is the best method?

Apple trees are no longer the garden-fillers that they once were. A wide variety of shapes and sizes is available.

Apples can be grown as small, freestanding trees or against a wall or fence. Cordoned Apples, trained against wires, make ideal 'hedges' between different parts of the garden. They can even be trained over an arch or pergola. Bush trees or spindle bushes can be grown in the vegetable garden or even in flower beds. The former is a rounded, open-centred tree, while the latter is pyramidal in shape.

A few varieties can be grown as a single pole, but the choice of fruit is limited. Cordoned Apples are best, as they take up little space and offer a range of varieties that will help with pollination, and crop over several months.

◄ Apple trees come in many shapes and sizes.

LAWNS

I want to create stripes on my lawn. How is it done?

You can create stripes on a lawn by flattening the grass in one direction, then repeating the process on a parallel strip in the opposite direction. This is very easy to do if you have a mower with a roller.

A cylinder mower with a roller behind the cutter is the best, but many rotary machines also have rollers and will leave distinctive stripes. Simply drive the machine over the lawn in alternate directions to create parallel lines, each slightly overlapping the previous strip.

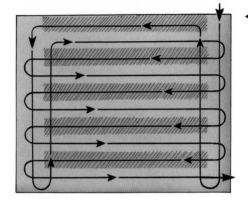

◄ Careful thought about the route to take will help produce perfect stripes. This plan can be adapted to most shapes of lawn, even irregular ones.

If you are feeling adventurous, you can also create more complex effects: a checkerboard pattern, for example, with lines running at right angles to each other so that squares are formed.

▼ Stripes epitomise the perfect lawn. The main requirement is a mowing machine with a roller.

▲ Grass seed can be spread by hand or a hired machine; the latter is best.

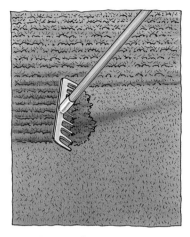

▲ Rake the surface so that most of the seed is lightly covered with soil.

▲ After raking, water the seed, and keep watered if the weather is dry.

Is it better to lay a new lawn from turf or to seed it?

As far as the finished lawn is concerned, there is little to choose between the two, although seed is likely to create a lawn with fewer weeds. However, there is quite a difference in the short term.

Turfing provides an 'instant' lawn that looks good almost immediately, and can be in full use in two or three months.

Unfortunately, it can be expensive. A sown lawn is much cheaper, but takes longer to establish and cannot really be used for heavy traffic in less than a year.

Seed does provide you with greater control of the grasses present, but together with its fine soil, it is likely to be stirred up by cats and dogs, and eaten by birds. Apart from mole damage, turf is usually trouble-free as long as it is kept watered.

▼ Lay turves on firmed soil, staggering them and butting them together.

▼ Gently firm the turves so that their roots are in contact with the soil.

▼ Fill any gaps with lawn sand or a sieved compost.

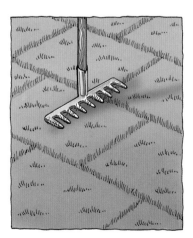

I want to create a lawn, but I have a young family who like to play ball games. Do I need any special sort of grass seed to cope with its likely heavy use?

The best looking lawns are made from grasses that are too soft to take a great deal of traffic, and which would certainly suffer if ball games were played on them. You will need a selection of tough grasses that do not look particularly lush, but that will bear the children's games without too much wear.

Although you can buy turf of specified grass, it is expensive, and you would be better off sowing seed. One of the main ingredients is the hard-wearing Perennial Ryegrass (*Lolium perenne*), but the mixture is also likely to contain softer grasses, such as Red Fescue (*Festuca rubra rubra*), for a better appearance. Precise

mixtures vary considerably, but the seed you require is usually specified as being for 'utility lawns'. Choose whichever seems the most appropriate.

▲ Lawns can be practical as well as decorative. Areas that are subject to heavy traffic or games can be planted with tougher strains of grass that will resist wear.

Which is best: a rotary or cylinder mower?

Ultimately, the choice will depend on your particular preference; both have their advantages and their disadvantages.

The best cut is provided by a cylinder mower; it looks neater and can be closer. However, a cylinder mower cannot cope with long or wet grass, and mowing in the spring, for example, is usually easier with a rotary mower. They also tend to miss stout, springy stems of grass.

Most cylinders have a grass collecting box, while many rotaries do not. However, rotaries are more versatile machines, but they do not produce such a fine finish. More thatch seems to remain in a lawn cut by a rotary machine than by a cylinder. Hover-type rotaries are good for cutting under overhanging plants and on banks.

Both types of machine need regular maintenance, but this is more critical with the cylinder mower, especially with regard to blade adjustments.

I am having great difficulty in eradicating moss from my lawn. How can I stop it coming back every time?

There are two parts to the answer to this question. Moss grows well in ill-drained lawns that are full of thatch, i.e. dead grass and moss which choke the living grass.

Remove this thatch and improve the drainage, and the moss is far less likely to return when you have killed it.

Rake over the lawn thoroughly so that all the dead material, plus

How essential is it to feed my lawn?

Grass, like all other living things, needs to be fed. In nature, vegetation dies back, decomposes and the nutrients are taken back into the soil to be used again. In the garden, most people remove grass clippings, and thus deprive the lawn of its returning nutrients. Keep this up for any length of time and the

▲ Rake the thatch out of the lawn to prevent it from choking the living grass.

▲ Aerate the lawn with a garden fork (left) or a hollow-tined tool (right) before treating with moss killer to improve drainage and prevent regrowth of moss.

as much moss as possible, is removed. Sweep this up or suck it up with the lawn mower, then aerate the lawn to improve its drainage. In light soils, this can be done by pushing a garden fork about 4in (10cm) into the ground repeatedly over the whole lawn. In heavier soils, use a special hollow-tined tool that takes out narrow cores of soil. Refill the resulting holes by brushing a mixture of

sieved compost (or peat substitute) and sharp sand into them.

Having improved the drainage and removed the thatch, now kill off the remaining moss and stimulate the grass into lush growth by applying a liquid or granular combined moss killer and lawn fertilizer. This can be carried out any time between late spring and autumn, when the soil is moist and the grass growing.

soil will become barren.

By fertilizing the lawn, you are replacing the chemicals that have been removed. Lawn fertilizers are specially formulated to stimulate root growth and create a green, leafy swathe. Some of them even incorporate moss- and weedkillers.

Lawns should be fed at least twice a year. The early feed should be rich in nitrogen to stimulate leaf growth, while the later one should be potassium-rich to keep the grass in good condition without making it too lush during the winter.

If the lawn is cut regularly, you can leave the short clippings to rot and be taken back into the soil. This must not, however, be considered if the clippings are abundant enough to create a thatch, which could choke the grass and encourage moss.

There is a small hollow in my lawn. How can I fill it without having to resow afterwards?

There is a simple method which should be carried out while the soil is moist but not wringing wet.

Make two slits in the turf at right angles to each other, to form a cross, using a turfing iron, lawn edger or sharp spade. The cuts should cross at the centre of the dip, with the ends of the cuts outside the area to be raised.

Gently peel back the turf, cutting under it with a spade if necessary, so that a square of exposed soil is opened up in the lawn. Add sufficient sandy soil or sieved compost to the hollow to raise the level of the soil, and firm lightly.

Fold the turves back over the bare soil and check the level; if necessary, relift the turves and adjust the amount of soil underneath, until the turves are level with the surrounding lawn.

A small hump can be treated in the same way, except that soil is removed rather than being added.

◄ To fill a hollow, start by cutting a cross in the turf, with the centre of the cross in the centre of the hollow.

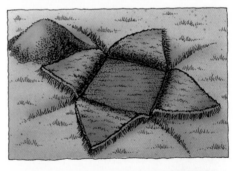

◄ Carefully peel back the turf and fill the hollow with sandy soil so that it is level with the surrounding soil.

◄ Replace the turf, check that it is level, and water the area thoroughly.

Moles are creating havoc with my lawn. Can I do anything about them?

You can buy a variety of smoke bombs and other deterrents, but these are not always successful, as the moles simply move elsewhere in the garden.

If you don't mind killing the moles, traditional traps are very effective. These are set in the runs. Also worth considering are humane traps, which catch the moles and allow you to remove them elsewhere. The most efficient, but expensive, solution is to employ a professional to poison them.

However, no cure is likely to last long, because any vacant territory is usually soon re-occupied by more moles. They will only burrow under lawns if there are worms to eat; killing off the worms will also remove the moles, but the only realistic solution is to learn to live with them and remove the molehills every morning.

▲ Cut around an area much larger than the damaged part.

▲ Lift the turf, making a level undercut, and slide it forward.

▲ Using a plank as a guide, trim off the damaged portion.

▲ Fill the resulting gap with a small piece of turf.

The edges of my lawn have become ragged and sunken in several places. I have tried filling the holes, but they still crumble away. How can I obtain a straight edge?

The edge of a lawn is always the most difficult part to repair, but the simple solution is to move the problem further into the lawn.

Remove a large section of turf, well beyond the damaged edge. Cut straight across the turf to remove the damaged piece and replace the undamaged portion so that the cut edge forms the new lawn edge. You will be left with a hole further into the lawn. This can be filled with the damaged turf and resown, or a completely new piece of turf. Not being on the edge of the lawn, it will soon heal.

A quicker alternative for slightly damaged pieces is simply to turn the cut turf around, moving the ruined edge into the lawn, then treat the damage.

WATER FEATURES

I would like to make a stream, but my garden is flat and there is no natural supply of water. Is there anything I can do?

While water can be moved around a garden by means of pumps and pipes, a slope is needed to get a stream to flow. The best solution is to construct a rock garden and incorporate a stream that runs from the top to the bottom. The slope does not need to be very steep; in fact, it will be better if it is not much above the horizontal,

otherwise the water will cascade down faster than the pump can replenish it.

If you prefer a steep slope, create a series waterfalls and slower (flatter) sections. Construct a 'spring' at the top so that the water appears to emerge from between the rocks, and let it trickle down into a pool at the bottom, from which it can be recirculated by a pump. If you do not want the pool, you will have to create an underground reservoir to collect the water for recirculation.

▼ A stream adds another dimension to a garden, especially if accompanied by the soothing sound of water tumbling down a waterfall.

I would rather create a natural pond than use a liner. How should I go about it?

Water features provide the perfect habitat for ferns and many foliage plants, creating a cool, lush picture.

▶ Creating a natural pond can be great fun, if somewhat messy. It should be lined with clay, and if you are lucky you may find clay subsoil when you dig out the pond. If not, you will have to buy some from a reputable merchant. Make certain that it is pure clay and does not contain stones or rubble.

When you have dug the pond, line it with the wetted clay, really banging it into place with your hands and feet so that it welds together with no gaps (do wear old clothes, as this is a dirty job). The traditional method was to run a flock of sheep into the pond to pound down the clay.

In a natural pond, the plants can be planted directly into the clay bottom. Tie a weight to each plant so that when lowered into the pond, the roots come into contact with the bottom.

▼ The layer of clay should be at least 4in (10cm) thick. Stones or other debris may allow water seepage, so remove them. Fill the pond with water as soon as possible to prevent the clay from drying out and cracking. The water will stay murky for several months, but eventually will clear.

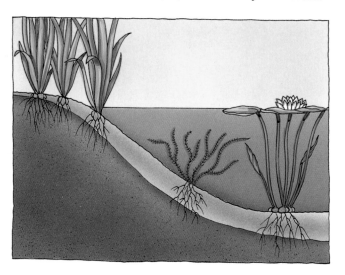

Is it true that pond plants always spread like wildfire?

Most plants that we grow in water spread quickly. This is not necessarily bad, as most are oxygenating plants, which produce oxygen for fish and other wildlife, and also help prevent the formation of algae and foetid water.

Fortunately, a little attention will help solve the problem. Remove some of the weed each month, using a spring-tined rake. Don't take it all, as the pond will suffer, just enough to prevent the pond from looking congested.

Marginal plants, which grow in the shallow water at the edge, are better behaved, and although some rapidly spread - Reed Mace (*Typha latifolia*) for example - plenty remain in clumps.

How can I plant a pond with a liner and no natural bottom?

The solution is quite simple: use baskets. Lattice-sided plastic pots are sold for this very purpose.

Fill the pots with garden soil or a soil-based compost (soil-less composts are likely to float away or decompose). Pot the plant in the normal manner, then cover the top of the soil with a 1in (2.5cm) layer of grit to prevent the contents from floating off.

Thread strings though the lattice and use them to lower the pot into the water, withdrawing them once the pot has been positioned.

▲ Clumps of yellow Candelabra Primula and Blue Poppy on the edges of a pond.

▼ Remove over-exuberant pond weed with a spring-tined rake.

◀ Use special lattice-sided pots for planting in ponds.

◀ Line the pot with hessian to prevent the compost from trickling out.

◀ Place the plant in the pot, and cover the compost with a layer of gravel to prevent it from floating away.

◀ Thread long strings through the pot. Two people can stretch these across the pond and lower the basket into position. Then the strings can be withdrawn.

A wide range of flowering plants enjoy boggy ground. They will provide a colourful picture even during dry summers, when ordinary borders are crying out for water.

▲ I don't want a pond, as I have young children, but I would like to make a bog garden. Can you give me a few pointers?

Water-loving bog plants are very attractive, so it is a good idea to have somewhere in the garden where you can grow them. This is not difficult to achieve, even in a dry garden. In effect, you need to create a pond, but fill it with earth instead of water.

Dig a shallow hole, 18-24in (45-60cm) deep, and line it with a butyl or polythene liner. Pierce a few holes in the liner so that it

I only have a small garden, but I would like a pond. Is this possible?

You can create a pond of any size, even as small as 12in (30cm) or so across. However, the smaller the pond, the more attention it will need, both to stop it drying out and to prevent the plants from taking over.

A very small pond is best constructed as part of a formal structure, such as a patio or wall, rather than as a natural-looking feature. A wall spout trickling into a

does not retain too much stagnant water. Back-fill the hole with earth, preferably mixed with plenty of fibrous organic material, such as shredded bark or leafmould.

If the bed is watered regularly, either by rain or by hand, the liner will retain enough moisture for the soil to remain permanently moist. In wet areas, a deep bed of organic material will be sufficient; no liner will be needed.

▼ Line the area of the bog garden with a normal pond liner.

▼ Make a few holes in the liner so that excess water drains away.

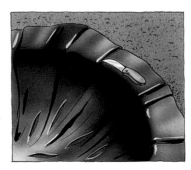

▼ Fill the liner with a moisture-retentive mixture containing well-rotted humus.

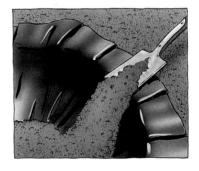

▲ Even the smallest garden can have a water feature such as this.

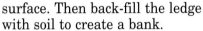

◄ The edges of liners detract from the appearance of ponds. Ensure that they are well covered with overhanging rocks, or bury them well into the bank.

small pond will keep the water fresh and aerated, while providing an attractive feature. A natural-looking pond can be as small as 6ft (1.8m) or so long, but do not grow vigorous plants in it.

I want to make a pond, but I hate the appearance of the black liner around the edge. How can I prevent this?

The obvious answer is to hide it, but that may not be as straightforward as it sounds. When making the pond, create a wide ledge at least 12in (30cm) deep around the outside of the hole, fold the liner into this, bringing the edge nearly to the surface. Then back-fill the ledge with soil to create a bank.

Alternatively, bring the liner to the surface at the edge of the pond and tuck it under stone or concrete slabs. This method can also be used when renovating an existing pond. Place the slabs so that they overhang the water slightly (not too far, as someone may stand on the edge and tip into the water) to cover the liner. This method is not totally satisfactory, as the liner may still be seen, but it will not be so obvious if the pond is kept full of water and marginal plants are grown.

▼ To help disguise a liner, bury it into the bank just above water level.

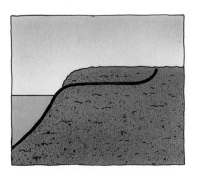

▼ If the pond is set in a patio, the liner can be hidden by overhanging paving.

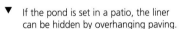
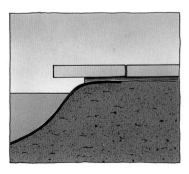

▼ Even in a lawn, it is a good idea to use overhanging slabs.

Is it a good thing to put fish in a pond? I have been told they are destructive to other wildlife.

Fish can be an essential ingredient for a pond. They add colour and movement, and are a constant source of pleasure.

▶ Destructive is probably too harsh a description, but like other animals, fish have to eat to live. Most consume a mixture of plant material, small insects and larvae. This can be a bonus, as it reduces the number of mosquitoes whose larvae hatch in the water. On the other hand, fish eat dragonfly larvae: insects that are well worth encouraging.

In the average pond, as long as it isn't overstocked, the benefits outweigh the disadvantages. To

calculate the ideal number of fish, allow 2in (5cm) length of adult fish per sq ft (930 sq cm) of the pond's surface.

Every summer my pond turns green. What can I do about it?

The leaves of Waterlilies (*Nymphaea*) shade the pond, helping to reduce the presence of sun-loving algae. Fish also welcome the cool shade.

▶ Many gardeners face this problem, which can be frustrating. The cause is algae. You can treat algae with an algicide, but it is much better to try to cure it by natural means first.

Algae needs plenty of sunlight and carbon dioxide, both of which can be reduced by providing the pond with plenty of oxygenating plants. They produce shade, and oxygen, as well as taking up a lot

of the minerals on which the algae feed. Waterlilies (*Nymphaea*) are particularly effective, as they shield the water from the sun, while Canadian Pondweed (*Elodea*) is a good oxygenator.

A fibrous form of algae, known as Blanketweed, will cover everything. It can also be cleared with algicide, but try restricting its growth first by hooking it out with a spring-tined rake, or by winding it around a pole. This will not eliminate it, but should stop it from becoming a nuisance.

You can remove Blanketweed and other algae with an upturned spring-tined rake, or by twisting it around a pole.

▶

CONTAINERS

I like the idea of window boxes, but are they safe, particularly on upper window sills?

The safety of a window box will depend on the precautions you take. A box simply placed on a window sill may look safe, but it can be dislodged by a high wind, or one of the eddies that such winds produce around buildings.

You should be able to fix some screw-eyes in the wall or window frame, then connect wires that either pass around the box or are attached to it. From time to time,

check that the wires are still secure at the wall and the box.

Another aspect to check is that the window sill is strong and secure enough to take the weight of the box. Never put a box on a rotting sill for example. If you are in any doubt, you can still have your box by fixing it to brackets attached to the wall.

Periodically check that the box has not cracked or rotted. Terracotta and ceramic boxes may crack in frosts, especially if the contents have frozen solid, putting great pressure on the sides.

▲ Make certain that all window boxes are well secured.

▼ Colourful window boxes can lift the appearance of a dull building.

What sort of compost should I use in my containers?

A simple, yet effectively planted, container that can be used in many places around the garden. Apart from watering, it needs little maintenance.

One of the most effective ways of using containers is to arrange them in groups. In this way, the display can be changed as plants come into, and go out of, flower. It also allows you to accommodate plants that like different soils.

▶ This will depend on your own preference as much as anything, but there are a few guidelines.

For hanging baskets, window boxes or containers on a roof garden, weight should be taken into consideration, and a soil-less compost is the best bet. However, for general use, a soil-based ▼ compost, such as John Innes No 2 or No 3, will be best. These are easier to re-moisten if allowed to dry out, and are less prone to overwatering, as they drain well.

Soil-less composts must be kept moist, as they are very difficult to re-moisten. Standing the container in water is the best way of coping with this problem.

If you want to grow Heathers (*Erica*) or Rhododendrons, use an ericaceous compost, which will not contain lime. Special water-retentive composts are available for hanging baskets.

Which is the best kind of container for Strawberries?

You can grow Strawberries in any container, including individual pots and even plastic growing bags. Special Strawberry pots are also available, which allow you to grow several plants together.

The simplest Strawberry pots are like herb pots: terracotta containers with holes in the sides for the plants. The more complex types are designed to be stacked on top of each other to build a tower of pots. The individual sections are rotated so that a series of 'balconies' spirals upwards, each containing a single

Which is the best method of planting containers?

Place some crocks or gravel in the bottom of the container to ensure good drainage, then add a layer of compost. For a single plant, hold it in one hand while trickling compost around it with the other, firming with your fingers. Tap the container to settle the compost, then water.

For larger containers and several plants, fill with compost and lightly compact by hand. Scoop out small holes and insert each plant, firming them in as you go. Level the surface and tap the container to settle the compost, then water. An attractive finish can be achieved by top-dressing the container with a layer of grit.

◀ Place crocks or gravel in the bottom of the pot to aid drainage.

◀ Fill the pot to a level just below its rim with a good potting compost.

▲ A simple way of growing Strawberries is to put several plants into one wide pot.

plant. Some towers can be suspended like baskets.

When watering Strawberry columns of any sort, make certain that all the plants receive water.

◀ Set each plant in its hole, firming as you go. Water-in and top up if necessary with more compost.

◀ Cover the top of the compost with a layer of grit or fine stones, keeping the level just below the rim.

Containers are ideal for growing herbs, especially where space is limited. Placing them outside the kitchen door, or on the window sill, means that they will always be within easy reach. ▶

Which herbs can I grow in a container on my patio?

If the container is large enough, you can grow virtually any herb, but most proprietary herb pots are only large enough for the smaller plants, such as Parsley and Basil. These containers often have pockets in the side, allowing you to grow a wide variety of herbs.

If you have borders nearby, you can grow larger herbs, such as Rosemary and Sage, in them, but there is no reason why you should not grow these in pots as well, preferably individually, as these plants can become quite large.

Bay trees make very attractive container plants. This newly-planted specimen will soon grow into a fine, large shrub. ▶

Are hanging baskets difficult to maintain?

Growing plants in containers of any sort is probably the most labour-intensive form of gardening. They must be watered and fed regularly, while the plants themselves require physical attention, such as deadheading. The work is not difficult; just time consuming.

Baskets must never be allowed to dry out, which means they should be watered at least once a day; twice or even three times on really hot summer days. You can suspend them from pulleys so that they can be lowered for watering, or you can buy a special bottle pump with a long, hooked lance, which will enable you to water the

How frequently should I water my containers?

Containers dry out very quickly, especially if they are made of terracotta, as moisture evaporates from the sides of the pot as well as the surface of the compost. Combining peat or peat substitute with the compost will help to retain moisture, but don't use too much, as the plants may become waterlogged. It can also be difficult to re-moisten.

You can buy a special water-retentive agent to add to the soil to improve water retention. Indeed, some composts, such as hanging basket compost, can be purchased with it already incorporated. However, most containers will be filled with ordinary potting compost, which

▲ To make watering and maintenance easy, you can hang baskets from a pulley system.

▲ Special watering devices with extended nozzles simplify watering baskets above head height.

basket from the ground. Using pulleys also allows you to lower the basket for deadheading and general tidying. Replace any spent plants with fresh ones.

Because of the constant watering, nutrients in the compost will quickly be washed away, so you must apply a liquid feed at least once a week.

will need watering at least daily, and more often in hot weather.

It is possible to rig up an automatic irrigation system, either with a drip feed or a time control

that turns on the water at fixed intervals. Such a system will be particularly useful if you go away on holiday and do not have anyone to water for you.

▼ This magnificent display will need constant watering to keep the *Impatiens* at their best.

▼ Automatic watering systems are useful if you are out at work all day or go away on holiday.

I am tired of growing bedding plants in containers. Can you suggest something different?

There is no need always to use flowering plants in containers. Foliage plants can also be very effective.

▶ Bedding plants are popular for use in containers because they are colourful and flower over a very long season. However, many other plants can be chosen, although they may have a more subtle appearance, and their flowering is likely to be for a short period. This may not be a problem, as the containers can be moved out of sight and others moved in.

Perennial plants will do well in tubs as long as they are not too congested and are regularly watered. Statuesque plants, such as Bear's Breeches (*Acanthus*), are particularly good, while large clumps of blue or white *Agapanthus* can be very effective.

It is not necessary always to use flowering plants either; foliage plants can also be grown. Hostas, for example, will provide interest for a long season. Shrubs and small trees can be grown as well, the classic example being the Bay tree (*Laurus*).

Can anything be used as a container, or are there things to be avoided?

Virtually anything can be used as a plant container - with a few provisos. Never use containers that have held chemicals. Even if you wash these thoroughly, traces may remain that could kill or maim your plants.

Make sure the container has drainage holes in the bottom; you should be able to drill or burn these in wooden or plastic pots. With care, you can suspend a normal plant pot inside a container with no drainage holes so that excess water trickles into the latter. Make sure that the outer container is large enough to hold the excess, otherwise the inner pot will soon be standing in water to the plant's detriment.

Only use pots that enhance or, at least, do not detract from the plant. A plastic food container with writing all over it will do little for any plant.

If you want to use ▶ a container that has no drainage holes in it, suspend the plant in an ordinary flower pot so that excess water falls clear of the plant roots.

PESTS & DISEASES

Are wasps garden pests? If so, how do I get rid of them?

In theory, wasps should be the gardener's friends, as they are scavengers and clear up quite a lot of debris; they even attack pests such as aphids. However, they also attack fruit, particularly if it has been damaged already by birds. Of course, they can cause nasty stings as well, and working near a nest can be dangerous.

There are several proprietary wasp killers on the market, but traditional insecticides, such as derris, work perfectly well. In the evening, when activity around the nest has subsided, squirt a

quantity of the powder into the nest entrance. Activity should have ceased by the next morning. Check the nest ten days later, as more larvae may have hatched and the activity started again. Repeating the treatment should solve the problem completely.

◀ If a wasp nest is easily accessible, you can deal with it yourself by puffing wasp killer into the entrance of the nest. Make sure you follow the manufacturer's instructions.

▼ Although wasps are a nuisance, as here, they can also be beneficial by destroying other insect pests.

I don't like to employ chemicals in the garden. Is there any way that I can avoid using modern insecticides and fungicides?

Hoverflies are among the beneficial insects in the garden. Their larvae eat large quantities of greenfly. You can attract them by providing plenty of nectar-rich flowers.

▶ In the main, modern insecticides and fungicides are efficient and safe. However, increasing numbers of gardeners are refusing to use them, except as a last resort.

Although biological control is gaining in popularity, many gardeners are turning to more traditional methods. One of the simplest is to create a diversified garden, which attracts predators as well as pests. If you only have Roses in the garden, you are bound to suffer from aphids, but if you have plenty of nectar-bearing plants as well, there will be hoverflies and ladybirds to help control the aphids.

Good hygiene in the garden also helps: remove rubbish that can harbour pests, especially slugs, and burn diseased material. If air can circulate freely between plants, the risk of certain fungal diseases will be reduced.

Sometimes physical methods can be used: you can remove caterpillars by hand and cover plants with nets to prevent butterflies from laying their eggs. Another traditional method is to use organic-based pesticides, such as soft soap, quassia, derris and pyrethrum, although they can be indiscriminate in what they kill.

Good hygiene, such as removing all decaying vegetation, will help reduce the population of garden pests.

Covering vegetables with netting or horticultural fleece will prevent birds from attacking the plants, and butterflies from laying their eggs.

I am rather suspicious about the so-called organic control of pests and diseases, and would rather rely on chemicals. How can I use them safely?

Many gardeners still use chemical controls, particularly as a last resort when all else fails. One of the objections to them is their safety. However, if used sensibly, they should be perfectly safe.

The first and most important rule when using chemicals is always to read

I have heard that there is nothing I can do about virus infections. Is this true?

Unfortunately, it is, at least as far as a cure is concerned. However, you can take preventative measures to reduce the likelihood of a virus infection occurring, or to prevent one from spreading.

Virus infections show up as discoloured foliage, often with yellow variegations, and as distorted stems and foliage. If found, the affected plant should be dug up and burned immediately. This will prevent it from spreading to other plants.

Such infections are introduced through wounds in the plant, so be careful not to damage plants through careless handling. They are frequently carried from one plant to another by sap-sucking insects, such as aphids, so try to keep these under control.

◄ Many Tulips have striped flowers (known as 'broken Tulips') due to virus attack. However, this is considered decorative rather than troublesome, and the plants are not destroyed.

While most plants with virus infections should be destroyed, a few are considered to have benign infections. The variegations on striped Tulips, for example, are caused by virus infections, but are considered to be 'safe'. Some variegated foliage plants are also formed in this way.

▼ Mosaic virus is usually harmful, and the distorted plants should be destroyed. Occasionally, when it does not unduly harm the plant, the effects are considered to be ornamental.

the instructions. Never use them other than as recommended, and never exceed the dosage. Always wear protective clothing, including goggles, mask and gloves. Thoroughly wash the equipment and yourself after use. Store both chemicals and dispensing tools as recommended, out of the reach of children.

Finally, only treat the affected part of the plant, unless recommended otherwise. If there are aphids on the shoot tips, spray them alone, not the whole plant.

Snails and slugs are causing a lot of damage in my garden. How can I control them?

One night of slug damage can reduce beautiful foliage to tatters. Hostas are particularly prone to attack.

▶ Snails and slugs are probably the gardener's worst enemies. In a night they can reduce prized plants to tatters. Although you can combat them with slug bait, many gardeners are against this, as it can poison other creatures, including pets and birds.

The simplest method of dealing with snails and slugs is to go out at night with a torch and pick them up. Then either kill them by dropping them into a jar or bucket of soapy water, or transport them somewhere else where they will not cause a nuisance. Doing this for several nights running will reduce the population to an acceptable level.

▲ Saucers, filled with beer and set in the ground, attract slugs, which then can be disposed of.

▲ Upturned grapefruit skins provide the slugs with daytime shelter, allowing you to collect them.

Alternatively, you can try old-fashioned tricks, such as leaving out saucers of beer to attract them, or putting out upturned grapefruit shells and checking them in the morning for slugs. There are organic slug baits on the market that are reputed to kill only slugs and snails. A biological control is also available, but it is expensive.

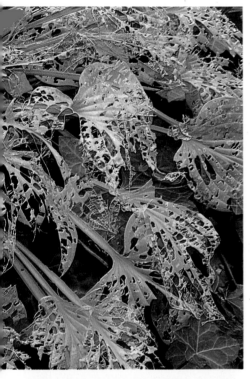

I keep hearing about the biological control of pests. What is it, and can I use it?

Most insect pests have a natural predator that hunts and lives on them. Biological control makes use of this fact by providing the gardener with predators to deal with pests. They are selected so that they do not attack anything other than the chosen pest.

Although biological control works best in a closed environment, such as a greenhouse, it is being used increasingly to good effect outside. Once released in the greenhouse or garden, the predator devours all of the pests. Then it dies through lack of food, but the cycle can be repeated the next time there is an outbreak.

You can order the relevant predator at a garden centre, and when the time is right for release, it will be mailed to you. The release date depends on various conditions, including temperature. There are different methods of releasing the predator, but often a sachet is simply emptied into a can of water and watered onto the affected area or plants.

▲ Mealy bugs intent on destroying a shoot. Spraying is often ineffectual against these pests, as the chemical cannot adhere to their waxy coats. Biological control, however, is much more successful.

◀ White fly, seen here on the underside of a leaf, are particularly troublesome in greenhouses. Biological control is a very effective form of attack against them.

I have lost a number of Primulas, which have wilted. On examining the remains, I found that the roots had been chewed through and there were several small, cream, horseshoe-shaped grubs in the soil, which I assume were responsible. What are they and what can I do about them?

Your plants are suffering from the ravages of vine weevil grubs. This is one of the worst pests in the garden, as there is little you can do about it.

Adult vine weevils chew holes in leaves, which is a nuisance, but not fatal. The grubs, however, do much more damage by chewing

Earwigs are one of the main pests of Dahlias, but they can be trapped in flower pots on top of canes.

Stuff straw or screwed-up newspaper into the flower pot and place it, upside-down, on a cane among the flowers. The earwigs will use the pot as daytime shelter and can be disposed of.

▲ **Every year the petals of my Dahlias, and several other plants, have been reduced to tatters. What can I do about it?**

▶ The cause of this problem can nearly always be attributed to earwigs, which come out at night to feed on petals and buds. You can deal with them by spraying, but most gardeners prefer to capture them.

The traditional method of catching earwigs is to fill a flower pot with straw or newspaper and set it, inverted, on a cane among the affected plants. After a night's feeding, the earwigs retire to the pot to sleep away the day. The gardener can then destroy the contents of the pot, including the

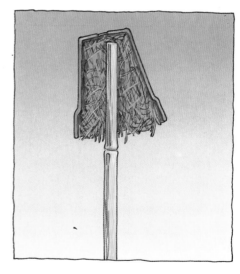

earwigs, and set it up again. After a few days, the problem will be reduced considerably. Use several pots for a large area of plants.

through the roots of many different plants, including Primulas, Geraniums, Cyclamen and Strawberries.

Once considered to be pests confined to the pots in greenhouses, vine weevils are now causing considerable damage in the open garden. Currently, there is no available chemical that will kill the grubs. HCH can be used to reduce the number of adults, but this is not particularly effective.

One efficient, and unusual, method is to allow chickens to roam through the beds in winter, scratching up and devouring the grubs. Another is to dig the affected area, sifting through the soil and removing every grub you can

▲ Vine weevils are among the worst pests in the garden, being difficult to combat.

find before replanting. There is a biological control, but this is only really effective when used in greenhouses.

Wherever I dig in my garden, I turn up lots of worms. Are they harmful, and should I use one of the wormkillers available in garden centres?

Worms are very beneficial to the structure of the soil and should not be harmed. Their tunnelling helps keep the soil drained and aerated, while they will consume and carry humus lying on the surface down into the soil. This is an excellent way of fertilizing the soil and improving its structure.

The wormkillers you see in garden centres are aimed at those gardeners who want perfect lawns without any trace of wormcasts (the little piles of soil left on the surface by worms). However, the

◀ Worms are very beneficial to the garden and should not be killed. However, gardeners who find wormcasts on their lawns unsightly, may wish to discourage them in this area.

good done by the worms far outweighs the minor inconvenience of regularly brushing off the wormcasts.

Some of my plants develop double stems, often with multiple heads where normally there should be one. What causes this, and what should I do about it?

Sometimes ugly stems appear where it seems that more than one stem have combined. These fastigiate shoots are not diseased, and there is no need to remove them unless you do not like their appearance.

▶ This is a natural process called fasciation. The cause is not known for certain, but it appears to be the result of the young growing tip becoming damaged in some way; perhaps due to sudden changes in temperature, or physical damage, such as being trampled. Normally, it only affects the plant for that year, and it cannot be transmitted like a disease.

You can throw affected plants away if you find the condition ugly, or you can wait until the following year when they should be back to normal. Although it is often said to be related to modern releases of radiation, there are plenty of records of the phenomenon that date back long before man started to play with nuclear materials.

A flower may double up with a second bloom or a leaf, such as in this Rose. It is not serious, and there is no need to take any action.

▶

SOIL & WEED PROBLEMS

I want to grow Heathers, but I live on a chalky soil. Is there anything I can do about it?

Heathers (*Erica*) are notorious in that they need an acid soil in which to grow. Nearly all will die at the mere hint of chalk. There is very little you can do to pure chalk to counteract the alkalinity; some remedies may last for a short time, but generally they soon break down.

Fortunately, there are one or two Heathers that will grow on chalk. *Erica carnea* is one, while the winter-flowering *E.* x *darleyensis* is another. If you want to grow any of the many other species and forms, the best way to do it is to grow them in containers, such as large tubs, filled with an ericaceous (acid) compost.

You could try digging a pit and filling it with acid soil, but even if this is lined with polythene, eventually the chalk will leech through and kill the plants.

▼ *Erica carnea* 'Springwood Pink' flowering in mid winter. This Heather will grow on chalk.

Is it possible to get rid of weeds without using chemicals?

Increasingly, gardeners are looking for ways of clearing areas of weeds without resorting to chemicals. The traditional methods of digging, hoeing and hand weeding are by far the best.

When digging a new or infested bed, remove every piece of root that you find. Leave the bed fallow for as long as possible, and remove any weed as it appears above the

▲ You can smother weeds with old carpet, laid face down.

▲ Regular hoeing will reduce the incidence of annual weeds.

surface. In this way, you will clear the bed efficiently.

Regular hoeing will remove annual weeds, but will have little effect on the more persistent perennials. Having said that, you can wage a war of attrition by hoeing as soon as any weed shows above ground. Eventually, this will starve even the most persistent weed, as all must receive light through their leaves to make food. Excluding light from the soil will have the same effect. Cover the plot with black polythene or an old carpet. It will look ugly, but it will starve the weeds out.

In some soil testing ▶ kits you mix the soil with a liquid in a small test tube. The liquid changes colour to indicate the pH of the soil: yellow/orange if acid; bright green if neutral; and dark green if alkaline.

When is the best time to dig the soil?

Although you can dig the soil whenever you wish, the best time is in the autumn. This will allow the rain and frost to break down the soil during the winter, producing a fine tilth. If you top-dress with compost or well-rotted farmyard manure, the worms

What is soil testing, and is it worth carrying out?

Soil is a very complex substance, and to ensure that it is at its best for your plants, you can test for several factors. Then you can take action to correct any deficiencies.

One of the commonest checks is for the level of acidity/alkalinity (pH). To grow Rhododendrons, you need an acid soil (pH4-6), but for a general garden, it is best to be just on the acid side of neutral (pH6.5). You can also test for nutritional deficiencies.

Always take samples from several different sites in the garden to achieve an overall picture. Soil testing kits are relatively inexpensive, and are easy to use. Most explain how to remedy deficiencies.

and weather will work this in over the winter months.

In areas of high rainfall, however, constant rain in winter can compact loose soil, so it is better to wait until the drying winds of spring have begun to take effect.

Never dig when the soil is wet. You will do more harm than good, particularly in breaking down its structure.

◀ A well furnished rock garden built on a free-draining foundation. It is possible, however, to create such a garden on a heavy clay soil.

Ground Elder and Couch Grass are growing through my flower borders. Is it safe to use weedkiller on them?

You could use a weedkiller, but the spray is likely to drift onto other plants; a gel is better, but awkward to apply. Even if you can keep the weedkiller off other plants, the herbicide can be spread through root contact underground.

For best results, dig out all of the border. If the soil is crumbly, go through it carefully, removing every piece. Otherwise, leave the bed fallow for a year and spray as the weeds appear.

Meanwhile, the plants can be kept in another bed, but make sure that their roots do not contain any weed roots, as these will spread into their new location.

I live on clay. Is it possible to create a rock garden?

Alpine plants need free drainage, which is something that clay will not provide. However, you can construct a rock garden above the clay so that any excess water will drain away.

The rock garden should be built with a mixture of loam and grit, both of which will probably have to be brought into the garden if you live on clay. Incorporate a drain at the base of the rock garden so that stagnant water does not just sit on the clay. An alternative is to build a raised bed using the same principles.

▲ All wet soils will be improved by the installation of proper drainage. The initial cost and effort may seem excessive, but the long-term benefits will make it well worthwhile.

◀ Combat Couch Grass and Ground Elder by digging over the soil and removing as much as possible. If possible, leave fallow for a year, removing any pieces of remaining root as they sprout.

I have a clay soil; how can I make it workable?

After a wet winter, a clay soil can become completely waterlogged. It is essential to improve the drainage and the quality of the soil.

▶ The first job is to make sure that the site is free-draining, and that there are no stagnant pockets of water; lay a drainage system if necessary. Then dig in as much organic material as possible. Garden compost, well-rotted farmyard manure, spent hops or mushroom compost, shredded or chipped bark, and rotted grass cuttings are all suitable.

If the soil is really sticky, you can add gravel or sharp sand. This will help to break up the soil and improve its drainage. The fired pieces of soil left in a bonfire after you have burned pernicious weeds are also excellent for this.

Clay often produces a 'cold' soil. Adding organic material will eventually darken it, which means it will warm up more quickly in spring. To hasten this, add a small quantity of soot.

Top-dress hungry soils with well-rotted compost or other humus in the autumn. As well as enriching the soil, this will also act as a mulch.

The worms will take some down into the soil. Dig in the rest in the spring, but avoid disturbing the plants' roots.

Top-dress the surface with another layer of humus, any remains of which should be dug in during the autumn. Then repeat the process.

On my sandy soil, I find that plants wilt very quickly through lack of moisture during dry summers. How can I improve it?

The cure for this problem is almost the same as that for treating heavy clay. Sandy soils drain very quickly, at the same time leeching out any nutrients. If you incorporate as much humus in the soil as you can, this not only helps to retain moisture, but also provides a slow-releasing source of nutrients to feed the plants.

This type of soil is very 'hungry', and the humus will disappear rapidly, so you need to add more at least once a year. The best way is to top-dress with compost or well-rotted manure in the autumn, then dig this in during the early spring, adding another top-dressing when you have finished planting. Dig this in in the autumn and top-dress again, and so on.

I can't spare the time for constant weeding, and I have heard that a mulch will help. What is it and how do I use it?

Mulches are ideal for reducing the amount of work needed in the garden: not only weeding, but also watering. The principle is that a thick layer of material suppresses the weeds and prevents moisture from evaporating.

Mulches can be any material that does not contain weed seed. Shredded or chipped bark is one of the best mulches, but you can also use grass cuttings, compost or farmyard manure. Gravel makes a good mulch for rock gardens, while black polythene is also useful as long as it is covered with something else to disguise it.

Always make certain that the ground is thoroughly watered before you apply a mulch. Unless an organic mulch is thoroughly rotted, it will extract nitrogen from the soil as it breaks down. To counteract this, apply a nitrogenous fertilizer beforehand.

◄ Before laying a fibrous mulch, make certain that the ground is moist, as it is likely to absorb a great deal of initial rainfall, preventing the moisture from reaching the plants' roots.

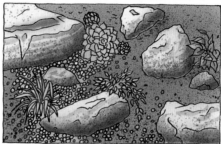

◄ This is not so important with gravel mulches, as used on rock gardens, as any rain will percolate easily through the fine stones.

What is loam, and how do I know if I have got it?

In gardening terms, loam is the ultimate soil. It is crumbly, fertile and moisture-retentive, but allows excess water to drain away. It works easily, even after heavy rain.

Loam normally comprises roughly equal parts of clay, sand and silt, with plenty of organic material. You will know intuitively if you have it, as it works so easily and produces good crops.

You can modify existing soil to produce a good loam, and any garden that has been worked over a long period of time will be very close to it. Regularly adding organic matter, such as compost and well-rotted manure, will help to bring about the change.

▲ You can improve the soil by working in plenty of well-rotted organic material.

INDEX